THE SPIRITUAL JOURNEY

TOWARD

A DANUBE 7 ORDINATION

Conversations with Companions of Conscience:

Rev. Dagmar Braun Celeste

Evelyn Elizabeth Hunt

Roberta Steinbacher

An Oral History
by Jacqueline K. Parker

For Bernie Schlager,
Best wishes at CLGS!
Jackie Parker
9-17-09

i

ISBN 978-0-9794000-1-8

Library of Congress Control Number: 2009926524

Copyright 2007 by Jacqueline K. Parker
Published by Constellation Press, 2009

Acknowledgments, with great appreciation, for:
Cover design and photo collages: CeCe Miller, Artistic Designer
and
Director/Choreographer of Spirit of Life Performing Arts in Dance,
Music, and Poetry
Danube Color Photo on cover: VikingRiverCruises.com/
OfficialSite online

Danube 7 Ordination photos, taken <u>on</u> the boat (June 29, 2002):
Courtesy of photographer, Erwin Wodicka. With special thanks to
Michael Mayr, and to copyright-holder, Christine Mayr-
Lumetzberger

Photo of Evelyn Hunt & Bishop Christine Mayr-Lumetzberger:
Courtesy of photographer, Michael Mayr

<u>New Women/New Church Newsletter</u> clipping (Summer 2003):
Courtesy of Women's Ordination Conference, publisher

<u>National Catholic Reporter</u> , Archives online (July 1, 2002):
John L. Allen, Jr., "Seven women 'ordained 'priests, June 29"

Private Collection photos of Dagmar Celeste, for:
Altar created in Discernment Retreat;
Dagmar on Retreat;
Gathering of Cleveland Faithful;
Roberta & Dagmar & the Venus of Willendorf;
Bishop Christine & Reverend Dagmar on the Danube
Private Collection of Kay Eaton, for:
Clipping, <u>Catholic Universe Bulletin </u>(Sept 1, 1972) &
Photo, C-WOC's "Women are Priestly People"
Finally, thank you to Evelyn Hunt for her care and kindness in
reading the manuscript.

Table of Contents

INTRODUCTION...1

THE SPIRITUAL JOURNEY TOWARD ORDINATION OF
DAGMAR BRAUN CELESTE 7

DREAM CATCHER, AN URBAN HERMITAGE 8

PEACE FORUM, SUMMER 2002 11

MISSION OF TYRIAN...13

MARGARET TRAXLER 16

SPIRITUAL WARRIORS..25

AFTER-EFFECTS OF ORDINATION ON THE DANUBE.............30

SAINT CECILIA'S STOLE 34

Mairéad Corrigan-Maquire, Nobel Peace Prize Winner...............39

INTIMATIONS OF "CALL" 43

"SOMETHING HAPPENED IN AUSTRIA" 46

THE DISCERNMENT PROCESS IN THE AMERICAN
HINTERLAND 54

EXCOMMUNICATION 62

THE "STEELING" TIME...65

ORDINATION ON THE DANUBE 75

THE DANUBE 7 80

THE COMPANIONS OF CONSCIENCE 83

PARTICIPANTS: 96

PROVENANCE: 97

APPENDIX 98

DAGMAR BRAUN CELESTE: THE FIRST AMERICAN
      ROMAN CATHOLIC WOMAN PRIEST, 2002   99

COLLAGES AND CLIPPINGS..103

NCR Online: Seven women "ordained" priests, June 29 (2002).113

     In ceremony they term "not licit, but a fact"   113

END NOTES 122

LIST OF COLLAGES AND CLIPPINGS
beginning p. 108

Elements of Altar created at Discernment Retreat 104

3 photos: Dagmar in hinterland; Cleveland group at Dagmar's Condo in Winton Place; Roberta and Dagmar at Paleolithic site in Austria 105

2 photos: The 7 women deacons awaiting ordination; Bishop Romulo Braschi laying hands on Dagmar 106

3 photos: Incensing the Ordinands; Dagmar's first communion (with Elli); Bishop Rafael Regelsberger hands Dagmar the cup 107

2 photos: Celebrants of the Ordination Mass; the 7, prostrate 108

4 photos: Granddaughter Eleanor assists with vestiture; Evelyn Hunt, WOC president, meets with RCWP Bishop Christine Mayr-Lumetzberger in Austria in 2006; Braschi & Dagmar embrace after the Danube 7 ordinations; the swan 109

2 photos: The Catholic Universe Bulletin (Sept. 1, 1972), photo (superimposed): Cleveland WOC 'presence' outside St. John's Cathedral as male priest is ordained (Nov. 3, 2006); *Jackie and Evelyn, New Mexico, 1994 110*

2 photos
RCWP Bishop Christine & the Rev. Dagmar on the Danube; New Women/New Church (WOC Newsletter, Summer 2003), First Year Anniversary of Danube 7 Ordinations: *RCWP bishops, Gisela Forster (Germany) and Christine Mayr-Lumetzberger (Austria) 111*

THE SPIRITUAL JOURNEY TOWARD A DANUBE 7 ORDINATION

INTRODUCTION

For those of you interested in women's history, Catholic women and their call to priesthood, this oral history provides a window into a particular personal journey. An attempt is also made to bring in references to influential women who inspired and shaped the thinking of Dagmar Celeste, including Roberta Steinbacher and Evelyn Hunt. The story and process focuses on the journey of Dagmar Celeste's call to priesthood in the Roman Catholic Church.

The discernment process had interesting beginnings, a period of germination and a two-week retreat before Dagmar left for Vienna and the Danube River ordination. Those of you familiar with the hierarchical Roman Catholic Church will appreciate the trepidation involved in this process. It is our hope that this oral history will enlighten many women to both the joys and the tribulations of women who walk forward through the 'flames' of patriarchal institutions to follow their inspirations and calls to service in particular ways. For those of you who have your own stories, we encourage you to tell them via oral histories or other published writings so that women in history may not be overlooked and forgotten. We need your stories. Young women need your stories.

For all the particularity of our own trajectories, there is the common experience of many women in the post-World War II world. In the American context there was the Civil Rights ferment, backed by court and legislative landmark achievements. Breakthrough ordinations of Protestant women began in the 1950s, including Episcopal women, ordained by male bishops acting prophetically in 1974. The denomination formally confirmed their status *after* the fact. The Episcopal women-priest ordinations played a part in triggering the Detroit meeting in 1975 of *vanguard* segments of Catholic women from religious orders, parish services, academic settings, who had already begun participating in post-Vatican II liturgical reform, ecumenical outreach, new scholarship, or peace and social justice advocacy movements. Dagmar and Roberta attended the 1975 gathering.

It was as if sections of John XXIII's encyclical, *Pacem in Terris* (1963), were written just for them!

> ¶ 13. ... *a system must be devised for affording gifted members of society the opportunity of engaging in more advanced studies, with a view of their occupying, as far as possible, positions in society in keeping with their natural talent and acquired skill.*

> ¶ 15. *Human beings have also the right to choose for themselves the kind of life which appeals to them: whether it is to found a family—in the founding of which both the man and the woman enjoy equal rights and duties—or to embrace the priesthood or the religious life.*

> ¶ 41. ... *the part that women are now playing in political life is everywhere evident... Women are gaining an increasing awareness of their natural dignity. Far from*

being content with a purely passive role or allowing themselves to be regarded as a kind of instrument, they are demanding both in domestic and in public life the rights and duties which belong to them as human persons.

¶ 48. ... *since all men are equal in natural dignity, no man has the capacity to force internal compliance on another ..... God...alone scrutinizes and judges the secret counsels of the heart.*

¶ 57. ... *the common good must take account of all those social conditions which favor the full development of human personality.*

¶ 163. *[the 'signs of the times' involves the]... task of establishing new relationships in human society under the guidance of truth, justice, charity, and freedom.*

The Vatican II conciliar documents continue:

From the Introduction to *Gaudium et Spes* [The Pastoral Constitution on The Church in the Modern World, approved by Paul VI, 1965]

¶ 3. ... the Church has always had the task of scrutinizing the signs of the times and of interpreting in the light of the Gospel. Thus, in language intelligible to each generation, she can respond to perennial questions... We must therefore recognize and understand the world in which we live, its explanations, its longings, and its often dramatic characteristics.

From *Lumen Gentium* [The Dogmatic Constitution on the Church, approved by Paul VI, 1964]

¶ 7. … *Through Baptism we are formed in the likeness of Christ: 'For in one Spirit we were all baptized into one body.'*

¶ 7. … *From Him 'the whole body, supplied and built up by joints and ligaments, attains a growth that is of God'. He continually distributes in His body, that is, in the Church, gifts of ministries in which, by His own power, we serve each other unto salvation so that, carrying out the truth in love, we might through all things grow unto Him who is our Head.*

¶ 18. *For the nurturing and constant growth of the People of God, Christ the Lord instituted in His Church a variety of ministries, which work for the good of the whole body….*

¶ 30. … *Everything that has been said above concerning the People of God is intended for the laity, religious and clergy alike.*

¶ 31. *The term laity is here understood to mean all the faithful except those in holy orders and those in the state of religious life specially approved by the Church. These faithful are by baptism made one body with Christ and are constituted among the People of God; they are in their own way made sharers in the priestly, prophetical, and kingly functions of Christ; and they carry out for their own part the mission of the whole Christian people in the Church and in the world.*

¶ 32. By divine institution Holy Church is ordered and governed with a wonderful diversity.... The chosen People of God is one: 'one Lord, one faith, one baptism'; sharing a common dignity as members from their regeneration in Christ, having the same filial grace and the same vocation to perfection; possessing in common one salvation, one hope and one undivided charity. There is, therefore, in Christ and in the Church no inequality on the basis of race or nationality, social condition or sex, because 'there is neither Jew nor Greek: there is neither bond nor free: there is neither male nor female. For you are all one in Christ Jesus.'

In the 1980s Dagmar found her "American" voice first in the feminist organizational spaces in Cleveland (The Women And Alcohol Project of WomanSpace; Of The Civic; Cleveland's Women Ordination Conference), then as activist First Lady during the eight-year term of her husband as governor of Ohio. (Evelyn was invited into the First Lady's 'core circle' and Roberta directed a state cabinet department).

Like others, Evelyn and Roberta had left their religious orders to live disciplined secular lives -- inspired, too, by a golden generation of Catholic women theologians, *periti*, as it were, for the American Catholic bishops in their many drafts of an ill-fated pastoral letter to women.

The summer courses offered by the Boston College Institute for Religious Education and Pastoral Ministry in the 1980s had great relevance for Evelyn's new awareness of transformations in women spaces in the greater society. (Her experience preceded Cardinal Law's appointment to head the Boston diocese.)

Before Roberta met Dagmar (at an event in the Trinity Episcopal Cathedral in Cleveland), she was an agent for Margaret Traxler in developing the ecumenical movement's outreach projects in the inner cities. Roberta institutionalized her role, later, as professor and director of the new Urban Studies Program at Cleveland State University.

Evelyn's work in the Office of Affirmative Action at Cleveland State prepared her in early retirement for national office and leadership as board member and president of WOC, the Women's Ordination Conference, and her role as behind-the-scenes strategist and planner for international conferences sponsored by WOW (Women's Ordination Worldwide), Call to Action, and NCMA (National Catholic Ministries Alliance).

It is this sense of "we-are-church," the everyday contexts of religious empowerment, to which this oral history is witness.

Dagmar Braun Celeste and Evelyn Hunt
Cleveland, Ohio, March 2009

THE SPIRITUAL JOURNEY TOWARD ORDINATION OF DAGMAR BRAUN CELESTE

Parker: This is November 24, 2002. We are at Evelyn Hunt's house in Cleveland Heights, Ohio in her TV room, and on the couches and chairs are Roberta Steinbacher, Evelyn Hunt, and Dagmar Celeste...

Dagmar: and Jackie Parker.

Parker: And Jackie Parker. We are going to start, finishing up where we left off on Tyrian, the Tyrian network. Where do you want to start, on that?

(Dagmar and Evelyn expanded on their earlier experience with urban and retreat ministries after attending the WOW conference in Dublin, and visiting the countryside of Brigid, in the summer of 2001. A recording of their immersion in Celtic spirituality, and the birth of "Tyrian, Inc." was made in December 2001. It is now known as part I of "Companions of Conscience," of which this conversation is part II.)

7

DREAM CATCHER, AN URBAN HERMITAGE

Dagmar: We left off with me describing the plan to build Dream-Catcher as a hermitage, a prototype, where down the line we can build more small retreat-type places on Kelleys Island. A year has gone by, and Dream Catcher has not yet broken ground, primarily because I don't seem to be able to find a contractor that I can afford. I've sort of set aside $100,000 to do it. But we are closer to breaking ground than we were a year ago (when the "Tyrian" tape was made).

Parker: Remind us what Dream Catcher is.

Dagmar: Dream Catcher is basically, a small, about 1,000 square feet place, that I am planning to live in next to my daughter, Noelle. I call it an "urban" hermitage. I'm going to start calling it an urban church! (laughter)

Parker: With a Catholic woman-priest on the premises!

Dagmar: But the idea was, we didn't have the resources to build the theatre and studio arts project on Kelleys Island, which is like a $10 million project, so I was going to build this one place, a studio, just to see what the expenses really are, and how green one can build such a place, et cetera.

The design is done; there are a couple of contractors that are competing. But none are coming close to the $100,000 budgeted amount.

I named it Dream Catcher after the native-American idea of the dream-catcher, that people hang over children's beds to catch the bad dreams, and only let the good dreams slip through. Hopefully, the symbolism will bear fruit.

The other thing in building it as green as possible, is to have some artists participate, some art brick work, some stained glass work … and maybe turn that into workshops. That is really down the line. First the walls and roof have to be up.

In the meanwhile, the rest of Tyrian has been kind of on the back burner, for me and Evelyn – because Evelyn got elected president of the Women's Ordination Conference (WOC) and I found myself preoccupied with ordination.

But we are having a board meeting coming up in December. A couple of new people are interested in participating: Richard Florida, who has written a book on "the rise of the creative class," who is going to be on the advisory board. And Yelena, who is a lawyer, and friend of Dennis Kucinich's, who is going to be willing to join the board. We don't have a lawyer right now on the board. A black woman in Columbus, who used to be in the First Lady's theology circle, who started a group called "women's work is ministry," Fran Frazer, is hopefully going to show up, if not on the board, then the advisory group.

Roberta is working at pulling together some proposals...

Roberta: I have a list of several Cleveland-based smaller foundations that are interested in the arts and culture piece, they seem to be different things to their minds! We are trying to show how they relate in the proposals that we are writing for them. Hopefully, one will fund the "Brigid Fest." We'll see. It's not great right now, the stock market being what it is. We're going to try that. I've been writing some of those. Dagmar is proofing them right now.

PEACE FORUM, SUMMER 2002

Dagmar: We did succeed in getting some money from a religious community who gave us a $2,000 donation toward the first Peace Forum, that we put on this summer. Mairéad Corrigan-Maguire[1] as the main speaker, that was Evelyn's idea. We met her in Ireland, and Evelyn thought it would be a good idea to invite her.

Parker: So there are a lot of irons in the fire.

Dagmar: Actually, there wasn't that great a participation. We did have Dennis, Congressman Kucinich.[2] The participation was not that great, but somehow we managed to make a $1,000 anyway. And Mairéad's lunch was very successful.

Evelyn: Yes, people liked the lunch. We have a bookstore here, which has a little room for special lunches. They provided the lunch, and her book! Her book, "Vision of Peace," they ordered for us. She also talked at the luncheon. We actually filled the chairs that we had.

Dagmar: About 30, 35 people.

Evelyn: Yes.

Dagmar: The main auditorium was, it's hard to tell because the Lakewood auditorium holds

	about 2,000 people. We never expected that! In fact, they promised to close part of it off, but they didn't and it looked kind of empty.
Evelyn:	We had about 250.
Roberta:	She was happy anyway. We had stickers, bumper stickers…
Dagmar:	It was a take-off on the notion of "God bless America"! We had Tyrian purple bumper stickers that said, "God bless us All" – with the world on it. (laughter)
Evelyn:	We did a lot of networking with the groups in Cleveland. We got mailing lists from different peace groups.
Dagmar:	We are now 'in the network' – two networks. The Northeast Ohio Peace Coalition and the Not in Our Name group. And a strategic planning group that meets at the Quaker House.

MISSION OF TYRIAN

Dagmar: Our mission in Tyrian is three-fold. To
            empower *creativity, healing, and peace.* We've
            done very well on the peace front. We are
            well-networked and we have done activities.

            On the *creativity* front, the fact that Richard
            Florida is willing to be on the Advisory, is a
            big plus. We haven't done much with artists.
            So this Brigid Festival, I decided we needed to
            focus on an artist. Can't think of her name
            now – she's done a piece of seven silk
            hangings, "the seven days of creation." She
            and Mary Garelick will develop a ritual based
            on a book that we picked up in Ireland called
            "The Seven Days of Creation" by Philip
            Newell.[3]

Parker: Evelyn, you've seen the hangings, haven't you?

Evelyn: Yes. Dagmar and I went to Notre Dame
            College in Cleveland. It has a little gallery in
            their library. The silk hangings were in this
            little gallery, in the front, so you could see the
            translucent quality on silk. You could see the
            lovely hues and pastels. Each hanging was
            representative of *women* creating, participating
            in the creation process.

Dagmar: Sophia, 'the seven faces of Sophia' would be
            another way of entitling it.

Parker: Besides the color on silk, do you see figures?

Dagmar: Yes. Woman figures.

Evelyn: Dagmar's arranging to use these silk hangings at the Brigid Fest coming up in 2003.

Dagmar: We've also decided, well, I've decided (laughter) to move Brigid from Lakewood Pavilion to Trinity Cathedral [Episcopal]. Trinity has just opened a new Commons, with a gift store and gallery space and a café where they serve fair-trade kinds of products. It costs the same, about $150, just like Lakewood Pavilion, except we don't have to worry about security. So, we'll see how that goes. It's a very imposing space, stained glass windows.

Roberta: You're talking about the Great Hall, yes.

Dagmar: The Commons space is going to be utilized in the sense that this woman's art will be exhibited in the new gallery. The gift store will be open, so people can shop there. Hopefully, we will be able to get the store to focus on Celtic stuff. We will have a few refreshments in the Great Hall; but if people want coffee or tea during the day, they can go to the coffee shop.

Roberta: That's a great idea.

Dagmar: It's going to simplify it. If that works, whoever
            takes it on next year won't have to do that
            much.

            We are going to give an annual award to some
            artist; and feature that work as part of our
            ritual. That's a whole new wrinkle. This
            woman is the first Tyrian artist-of-the-year.

Parker: Dagmar, you said you and Roberta met at the
            Cathedral?

Dagmar: It was a Schubert concert?

MARGARET TRAXLER

Roberta: No, it was Margaret Traxler[4].... I belong to this creation of hers called the Institute of Women Today. We would travel around the country talking about, first of all it was racism and the war, and then it was, when the (Vietnam) war ended finally, we started doing workshops on women's self-esteem, growing out of consciousness-raising. We'd do this around the country.

This one happened to be in Cleveland. It was sponsored by the local churches, to be an ecumenical, church-group type thing. Dagmar came with Anda Cook, whom we know very well now, and other friends that we still have from 1974, when we held the workshop here at Trinity Cathedral.....

: We would bring a team of social scientists and a lawyer to bear on this; we would talk about inequality, and those things we were experiencing.

Dagmar: It was basically Margaret Traxler, who got the financing from the Schubert family, right?

Roberta: Yes, some money from the family for the 'traveling workshop', as we called it. She had money from small foundations, and her own group back in Chicago, called the Institute of Women Today. It still goes on. I get the newsletter. But they don't travel anymore, they just stay in Chicago.

Parker: Roberta, how did you get connected with this?

Roberta: Margaret Traxler was my boss in the job I had and came to Cleveland to do.

Parker: What was that?

Roberta: "Project Bridge." It was an effort, starting in 1967, to try to get interracial programs going that focused on things outside of race, like housing, crime, areas where blacks were moving and whites were moving out in the late sixties. The aim was to get community leaders together from both races, to sit down and talk about our common problems, and try that way to get over these problems. It was right after the urban riots.

I came to Cleveland for that. There were five nuns who came from various places. I didn't know where I was going until two weeks before I was assigned Cleveland. We all came here, and did that for several years. Margaret Traxler was one boss, working for the Catholic Conference for Interracial Justice in Chicago, and the other half of it was the American Jewish Committee in New York. We had bosses from both places who would fly in and out and look at us.

Parker:	Let's focus on you a moment, Roberta. I think in some ways you seem to be Dagmar's alter ego. (laughter) You were in orders then, Roberta?
Roberta:	Yes…
Parker:	When did you go into orders?
Roberta:	I went in in 1953. I was just finishing up my degree, trying to find a job.
Parker:	Ph.D.? In what?
Roberta:	Psychology. Mother Superior saw this ad in a nuns' newsletter. She thought this would be a good idea. I answered the ad, with a letter to Margaret Traxler. She hired me without ever seeing me. She just said in her letter, "you're on!"
Parker:	Okay. Let's concentrate on Margaret Traxler for a minute. Dagmar has said that Margaret Traxler was one of the influential persons in her life.
Dagmar:	Yes, plus she died, just about the time I was trying to figure out whether or not to move ahead with this vocation. It is almost spooky. It's sort of like I had the sense that she was cheering us on. She herself had had a call to ordination. Supposedly there was a bishop who was even ready to ordain her, at some point.

Roberta: Yes, she told me that.

Dagmar: Because of her humility, I suppose. She decided it wasn't the right time for her to do it on her own, or by herself. I don't know. Maybe she was ordained, and we just don't know! I clearly had the sense that when she died, she passed the baton to us.

Roberta: To Dagmar, yes.

Dagmar: Robby, she called you.

Roberta: Robby, yes. Margaret was incredible. Humble, yes. But a fierce fighter in church matters that affected women, and the poor. Just fierce. She was Joan of Arc and they burned her at the psychological stake more than once. She led the deal against the Pope, how long ago was that? In Rome, she was marching. She had to be 70, then. She was holding up this huge sign, "Meeting *About* Us, *Without* Us!" (murmurs from the group).

                    I've forgot what the issue was. We'll have to remember what the occasion was. It was just about three years ago.

Dagmar: I think it was about wearing habits? I think it was the religious women…

Roberta: Three years ago.

Evelyn:	It was probably the Congregation for the Religious. Oh, NCAN? No?
Dagmar:	No, she started NCAN.
Roberta:	She started NCAN (National Coalition of American Nuns). She started Maria's Shelter -- she started two shelters for women in Chicago.
	(the other was Casa Notre Dame, both on the South Side. Apparently, she earned the support of Cardinal Bernadin and Mayor Washington for her ventures, including "Sisterhouse", founded to prepare women prisoners for the job market after release. *See* footnote, above).
Dagmar:	She was on the founding board of Mary's Pence.
Roberta:	She started Mary's Pence. That's the thing I was trying to think of. She started all of these organizations, then she would leave them, get it started and leave. Like many of us early on in the women's movement, she started striking out against the war, then racism, and then poverty. She ended up with women in prison, half-way houses for women coming out, these shelters.
Dagmar:	I remember seeing her on a television show, maybe Phil Donohue when he was still on in the morning. She was raising money for

Biafra. I never had done anything based on a television show. But after I was done listening to her on Biafra, I picked up the phone and called St. Edwards, and talked to Brother Charles Van Winkel who was in charge of relief in Cleveland and got together with him. We did a telethon. And ended up with enough money to build a hospital in Nigeria.

That was my first encounter with Margaret Traxler.

Roberta: That had to be in the early fifties.

Dagmar: I met her in person at Trinity Cathedral when I also met Roberta. She then joined the "core circle" meeting, my campaign core circle, that we had at Lesley Brooks Wells[5] house. She pretty much told me that she expected us to get elected. She told me she fully expected me to do something about women in prison once I became First Lady. And I did (during the Celeste administration, 1983-1991).

Parker: Let's back track again. You met Margaret Traxler in the sixties? Can you describe her?

Roberta: 1967. She was incredibly, incredibly generous. She was always there for whoever was in her presence. Just totally open to whoever was in trouble. She could just read you like a book, also. I think of those qualities, along with her pioneering spirit and *never* giving up, fight, fight…

Dagmar: She had short hair, round faced, she was
            attractive, but she was not imposing. She had
            very captivating eyes, blue or green. I think we
            have very similar eyes. She had a good sense
            of humor. But like Roberta says, she was very
            humble, the only word… self-effacing, almost.
            But not when it came to matters of
            importance. She was kind of self-effacing in
            her manner with people. When it came to
            issues, she was a dynamo.

Roberta: Probably like lots of women who were
            outspoken for justice. She never took credit
            for anything. She'd tell people where to 'get
            off'. She knew who the enemy was.

Parker: Can you give me an example?

Roberta: She would stand up to priests, she would
            stand up to bishops, the pope. It didn't matter.
            She would get on the radio, television, and say
            these things. And fight fiercely. She would
            have no hesitation. Say it like it was.

Parker: What part of the country did she come from
            originally?

Roberta: Mankato, Minnesota. That's where her
            mother house was. I met her mother. Her
            father died very young. Her father was a
            doctor.

Parker: Do you want to mention the name of the
            bishop who was her close friend?

Roberta: Murphy. I don't remember his first name.

Dagmar: You'd better find out because he's giving you
            money! He may have been from the
            Minnesota, too. Because this Jesuit who is
            supporting me now was a friend of Frank
            Murphy's. [6]

Parker: And the connection to your organization, Ev?
Evelyn: He left money to the Women's Ordination
            Conference. We give scholarships with that
            money to women who are studying for
            ministry in the Roman Catholic church. Same
            man.[7]

            He's the one who is also a friend of Donald
            Cozzens, who is a local priest. Don Cozzens
            dedicated his most recent book to Murphy.

Roberta: Oh, my God!

Evelyn: It comes around! (goes to bookshelf)

Parker: OK. What's the name of his latest book? This
            is now Don Cozzens.

Evelyn: It is "Sacred Silence: Denial of Crisis in the
            Church."[8] He says, "In Memory of P. Francis
            Murphy and Raymond Lucker: Men of faith
            and courage who dared to break the silence."

SPIRITUAL WARRIORS

Parker: Roberta, you have this marvelous connection with Margaret Traxler! She sounds a little bit like Dagmar describes herself somewhere (maybe back when you were ordained), as a "spiritual warrior." Dagmar, can you tell us about that?

Dagmar: I guess a spiritual warrior is somebody who is not afraid of 'powers and principalities', and is willing to risk her own life if necessary. But not someone who it willing to kill.

Parker: It's risk-taking. Roberta, you mentioned you wrote a psychological evaluation of Dagmar. Do you want to pick up on that theme?

Roberta. I'd forgotten it. Once she has studied the issue, as Dagmar does methodically, whatever she is going to do before she actually does it, and consults and discerns and all that – once she does that, she is not even thinking of consequences anymore. That's what I meant. Margaret and Dagmar are alike in that. As Dagmar was talking, I was thinking of "speaking truth to power" – they are both like that, without any fear of the consequences from the men who run the churches. If they are going to kick you out, they are going to kick you out. Margaret never hesitated to say what she had to say to get the truth out.

Dagmar: It's not that you're not afraid of consequences.
You are aware of consequences. You are fully
aware of consequences. And you are afraid,
too, at times. But not to the point of letting
yourself be deterred from something. If it's
going to happen, it's going to happen by
virtue of people struggling.

I have to say I haven't suffered particularly
heavy consequences for my beliefs, yet. This
excommunication is close; maybe my divorce.
With my divorce, I felt the pain intensely. But
with the excommunication, I am completely
at peace. Maybe it's a numbing process! It is
something of a different order after all.

I do think that people like Margaret, if you
look at this from the outside, you say 'Oh,
how brave, how courageous,' whatever. But I
think when you are doing it yourself, it is just
part of who you are, what you are. The
strength comes from beyond you. It doesn't
seem that big a deal.

Parker: What about your take on that, when you were
writing about her risk-taking?

Roberta: I agree with what she just said. You're much
more open and empathetic and into the
feeling of another going through that, than
when you are going through it yourself. She
would define it as something beyond yourself;
I might say it is adrenalin. (laughter)

Dagmar:	Battle-juice! Beetle-juice!
Roberta:	Therefore, when you've had something on your mind, gained clarity about the situation, you've said yes to it. The consequences will fall where they may. You're much more prepared, you don't really feel it when it comes. It's what happens.
	Margaret together with others fought a whole lot of national figures in this whole area of "choice." They signed that statement in the New York Times. They were all close to excommunication. They were required to recant. Mother superiors were all up in arms. That hurt Margaret a lot.
Parker:	This is the Call to Action?
Dagmar:	No, no; this was not Call to Action.
Parker:	What was it?
Evelyn:	It was a statement in support of women's choice. NCAN? Oh, choice for abortion?
Roberta:	A huge number signed the statement in the New York Times. All the nuns were in deep church trouble.
Parker:	Did Margaret stay within her order?
Dagmar:	Oh, yes.

Roberta: Yes, she stayed. She always said, "I'm not leaving."

Parker: And her order supported her?

Roberta: Yes, her order supported her.

Evelyn: There were a couple of other women from West Virginia who signed that. They were really pressured out of their order. But they continued to do the work that they were doing. They had a women's center in Charleston. They actually wrote a book about it.[9]

Dagmar: It's like Jeannine Gramick. She's been forced out of her order. She continues to do the work that God called her to do.

Parker: Which is a gay and lesbian ministry among Catholics. New Ways ministry.[10]

Dagmar: Gay and lesbian. I just think once you have a call that's clear, I don't know how you would give up on that.

             I mean, I keep saying if they could actually burn me at the stake, I probably wouldn't do it. I don't know. But then I think to myself, who knows? Maybe the power would just increase. Whatever it is that is helping you do whatever we are going through now, whether it is the fight on behalf of other women, or our own behalf, whatever it takes if it is a call, you will have it, you will get it. Presumably that goes on. No matter how far you push the envelope. God will provide whatever it takes for you to stay with it.

It's not one's own merit. I think the reason why Margaret came off as humble and self-effacing, was because she understood a lot faster than certainly I understood, that it wasn't her doing it. Once she had turned over her life to this higher power, then she was just providing the arms and the legs. I don't think you are taking risks, once you have a call.

Parker: So what Roberta called risk-taking, you mean 'being called'. What were you going to say, Ev?

Evelyn: I was going to say it reminds me of a prophet. I think these actions that Margaret Traxler, and many people in the women's movement, and Dagmar included, have taken are prophetic actions. Like God calling a prophet in the Old Testament, and the person saying, "who am I? I'm just a … why me?"

Dagmar: Well, you protest! (cell phone rings) Before it is clear that you got to do it! …

AFTER-EFFECTS OF ORDINATION ON THE DANUBE

Parker: In the file you are looking at, Dagmar, you
            say, "that if you didn't accept the call, you
            would have a broken spirit. But if you accept
            the call, the consequence might be Exodus."
            In other words, excommunication, and I
            suppose you mean isolation and casting out.

Dagmar: That is what excommunication is. Casting out
            from the community you are dealing with in
            Catholic circles. But the reality is, "so now,
            that is what has happened." I didn't spend a
            lot of time imagining it, although it was a
            possibility. It's a little bit like looking at death
            as a possibility of child birth. It is a possible
            consequence of going through a pregnancy. It
            comes to mind.

            I didn't dwell on it once it happened. It
            happened so fast. They gave us two weeks to
            recant. Then they excommunicated us. The
            day that I thought we were excommunicated,
            Evelyn and I were at a service at Mary
            Magdalene Church. Evelyn presented me with
            a hand-stitched stole from the local women's
            ordination conference people that had been
            embroidered by one of the pagan members of
            our community.

            It just so happened that the woman I'd been
            doing body work on was there.... We were
            under the statue of Mary Magdalene. We

30

couldn't have designed it!. Martha Church (a pseudonym), who was kind of a nemesis throughout the whole process, had organized the meeting!

Evelyn: The Magdalene meeting.

Dagmar: I handed Martha back the papers she had sent to the bishop who had inquired about me discretely. The whole thing just fell into place. And then I was still anonymous. So I had this period of time, about two months, when nobody knew.

Parker: Because your name was…

Dagmar: Because I had used the ordination name of Angela White. Nobody really knew, except folks close in who had been supportive. It helped kind of balance myself. I didn't get whiplash. After Natalie's wedding – I'd taken that name for the Danube 7 ordination because I didn't want to overshadow Natalie's wedding, not be able to take communion, whatever, or have the press invade that celebration – so I stayed anonymous until after the wedding.

            I knew the *Cleveland Plain Dealer* was going to come out with an article. So I got ahead of the *Plain Dealer* and prepared a story for the Associated Press. But before I gave it to A.P., I sat down with the bishop here in Cleveland.

He was cordial. He listened to the whole thing.

I thought he'd just show me the door the minute I mentioned what I was talking about. Because he's not supposed to talk about these matters! The pope had pretty much said that nobody in the Roman Catholic church could even discuss women's ordination. So when I say, "I'm here to discuss being ordained," I thought he'd say, "Thank you very much. Goodbye."

He asked, "How did this happen?" So I gave him a quick version of my call story. Then he just looked at me and said, "Well, now what are you going to do with it?" I said, "I suppose you are not going to give me a parish! I'll keep living my life. At some point it may be clear about what I'm supposed to do with this."

As cordial as he was, they jumped the gun immediately. The American bishops are much more cowardly then even the European bishops. They jumped the gun immediately. They put in the paper that I was excommunicated. That meant I couldn't even go in to a Catholic church, which was kind of far-fetched. At that point, I did get kind of ... wow, it's different, the resolve at one level, but it also threw a bit of terror into my heart. The way they went at this, very heartlessly, just looking out for their own well-being.

But unbeknownst to me, the excommunication was almost more necessary than the ordination. Part of what happened since the excommunication, the people who feel they have been excommunicated (and often aren't, even), and other people who are excommunicated for whatever reason, either because they are living out of wedlock, with somebody of their own sex, because they have remarried without annulling the first marriage, because they had an abortion, whatever the myriad of reasons are, they were the ones who started calling! It became very clear *who* I was ordained for.

SAINT CECILIA'S STOLE

Dagmar: It's still not clear, exactly, what I'm supposed
            to be doing. Every Sunday brings new insight.
            Today I went to St. Cecilia, and he introduced
            me from the altar. Secondly, the person who
            was doing the reading was the same person
            who I'm negotiating with for my Dream
            Catcher contract. Carlton Rush happens to be
            in that parish; he's a black gentleman who
            used to be the housing director for the city of
            Cleveland. Thirdly, the head of the diocesan
            commission for community action was there.
            Len Calabrese. And the woman who invited
            me to this place, that I'd never heard of 'til
            now, was a friend of Dorothy Day's. She's that
            age, a mother of one of the women who used
            to be a member of your community, she came
            to a book-signing event of mine last week that
            I was doing for the Ethical Society of
            Cleveland. They don't even have religious
            people in it, they're secularists. Here's this
            woman who came just because I was signing,
            because I was there. She came to this
            Unitarian church to meet me and to invite me
            to her parish….

Evelyn: Something about these circles here.
            Synergy.

Dagmar: Also, another priest invited me to his parish,
            despite the fact that I have been
            excommunicated. And after the service, I was
            downstairs having a cup of coffee, and these

34

women just collected in a little circle. It was just like in Saint Paul's time, this total group of strangers – and at this time I didn't even have my own name – and still it happened. I may talk about this a little bit later. But people did know who I was, because they welcomed me from the altar, to boot. They are all the active women in Saint. Cecilia's, the black woman Vivian is the secretary, and the white woman was the reader. Another young white woman was doing something else. Today they are celebrating the feast day of Saint Cecilia.

The last time I was at a Call to Action conference, I had this experience. I never knew who Saint Cecilia was in my life. But her feast day was on my daughter-in-law's birthday. I just found out about it. This young priest was there with another woman from his parish. He was wanting to buy this beautiful green stole with just music on it, no words. Instead of buying it for himself, he bought her (the woman from his parish) another stole, not a fancy one but a stole. I saw how he went back and touched the green stole. I said to him, "Is this something you would really want?" And he said, "I'm a great fan of Saint Cecilia, the patron saint of music." But I don't want to spend $150 for the stole, we are not a wealthy parish." That evening I thought about it: $150 is a little steep for me, too. I went back to this booth where they were selling vestments and stoles. The woman wasn't there (I was going to negotiate with her). So I left her a note, saying 'I'm interested in this stole. I cannot afford to pay $150, but I would be willing to pay $98. If you're interested in selling it, I'll come by tomorrow. She sold it to me for $98. (laughter) I bought it.

At that service, it was an interdenominational service with all kinds of people at the altar, you couldn't even tell who the priests were, he was in the audience and I gave him his stole. But before I had a chance to give him the stole, there was a nun in full habit across the aisle from me. She had a name tag, it said Cecilia. So we greeted each other. I said, "What do you know about Saint Cecilia?" because I knew nothing. She said, "I'm named after her. Her feast day is the 21st or 22nd of November." So when I gave him the stole, I said, "You had better wear this on Saint Cecilia's Day." He was like overjoyed.

He happened to be at Bishop Gumbleton's talk the other day. He was standing there with the guys. He just left those guys standing in their tracks and came and embraced me.

The point is, here's Saint Cecilia. Obviously I was meant to find out a lot about her way before I had a call to ordination. Here's this parish. I've got an East Side and a West Side parish that I can go to.

Parker: To back up, how were you introduced at Saint Cecilia's, as Father Dagmar, or Sister Dagmar?

Dagmar:	Just as Dagmar Celeste. This is interesting. Just like when I was First Lady of Ohio. The question came up, how do we introduce you? As Mrs. Richard Celeste? As Dagmar Celeste? Or just First Lady. I always said, "Dagmar will do." And I still feel that way. I think the whole idea – shall we call you Father – is the whole thing we are buying into. I have an email this morning where this guy makes the argument (this is a group called Catholicity, against women's ordination), that because women can't biologically be fathers, they can't be priests. (laughter)
Evelyn:	The language!
Dagmar:	But I've had as many women say, "Do we call you Father now?" Like they can't think of anything else but these hierarchical terms of either mother or father, when in fact we're supposed to be sisters and brothers. We're not even supposed to be shepherds; we're supposed to be sheep!
Parker:	You heard the lectionary reading today!
Dagmar:	But the point is, priests see themselves as shepherds; bishops see themselves as shepherds. No, we've got a shepherd. We've got a high priest. We really don't need priests. But we need a lot of women-priests to bring the whole hierarchy down, where it belongs.

Evelyn: Right among the people.

Dagmar: Right among the sheep. (laughter)

Evelyn: I've got sheep up there (on bookshelf); one of
               my favorite animals. (laughter). Right along
               with the ducks.

Dagmar: I don't know what they've got against the
               goats! (laughter)

MAIRÉAD CORRIGAN-MAQUIRE, NOBEL PEACE PRIZE WINNER

Parker: Let's go back to the Tyrian introduction. I want to hear more about Mairéad Maquire. Just tell us her importance. Is she an international figure?

Evelyn: Yes, she is. She's a woman from Northern Ireland. She has a family there. She's one of the women that started the resistance against violence in Northern Ireland in the early seventies. Her sister lost her spouse, I think.

Dagmar: And the children.

Evelyn: No, Mairéad adopted the children. Maybe she lost a couple of them. Mairéad had to take the children in and raise them at a certain point, because I think her sister died eventually, too.

            She was so enraged by this violence, this sectarian violence in Northern Ireland, and the impact on children and women and innocent people, that she organized a peace movement in Northern Ireland. She and some other folks, it wasn't just her, spearheaded the organization of thousands of people in Northern Ireland. They protested the violence.

Dagmar: And she got a Nobel Peace Prize. She is a Nobel Laureate.

Evelyn:	In 1976 she won the Nobel Peace Prize. Dagmar and I met her in Dublin at the Women's Ordination Worldwide (WOW) conference. She was a major speaker there. We were talking after she spoke and decided to get her information, her email, and how to get in touch with her. I think even then we were thinking about our Brigid Fest, and so forth.

Anyway, in emailing her, I asked her if she could be at the Brigid Fest in February the following year, and she couldn't come. Then she emailed back she couldn't come in February, but she had this window of time in June of 2002. She was going to be in New York with the Fellowship for Reconciliation doing some things, and that she could allow us to plan her into our schedule.

So we scurried around, really, as Tyrian, and began pulling together an event, which was her speaking to all the peace groups that we could get in June, the second week of June. She agreed to come and we organized this event. She'd give the major speech, and we organized the book-signing, and the lunch for the people that wanted to go to that.

Parker:	And substantively, what did she say that stirred you – or did she?
Dagmar:	She has an organization now called Peace People. This was pre-Iraq war attack; I guess we were already into Afghanistan. But

basically, she is almost soft-spoken but very, very convincing about the uselessness of violence, how it just doesn't accomplish even what those who perpetrate it imagine it should and does so much damage.

Evelyn: And she spoke of the need to bring people together on a human scale. She had a lot to do in Northern Ireland in bringing the children of both sides together. And is also having an exchange with youngsters in the United States. The idea of dialogue and working together to know one another on a human level. So it personalized the work for peace.

Parker: And we know that next year you are going to feature an artist and her silk screen panels?

Dagmar: That's for the Brigid Fest.

Parker: Oh, that's not for Tyrian; or is that the same thing?

Dagmar: Tyrian is doing two events at this point. One is the Brigid Fest on an annual basis. The Brigid Peace Fest. The other one we call the Tyrian Peace Forum. That one we'll do only whenever we can get a Nobel Peace Prize winner to come to town! Then we'll just pull that together.

Evelyn: Yes.

Dagmar: And the third thing that we are hoping to do is this creative retreat center on Kelleys Island . Basically, workshops and seminars and opportunities to empower creativity in-town and out-of-town. That's a lot more fluid.

Evelyn: Right.

Dagmar: Just between the two of us (Evelyn and Dagmar) we can barely keep those two events going. Roberta is helping to raise some of the money, but Roberta had not been able to do any of the logistics on pulling together the events.

Actually, the person who has helped the most on the Peace Forum is a person called Leatrice Tolls, who is a former student of mine from Kent State. She was very instrumental in pulling together a coalition of peace groups to co-sponsor the Peace Forum.

Until we have a little bit more money so we can pay a salary for somebody, it is pretty much Evelyn and me. Now with her responsibilities with WOC, it is pretty much me.

INTIMATIONS OF "CALL"

Parker: While this was going on, you were doing the
Tyrian Network, feeling your way through
that. You received a call to Austria, and that
set a whole new process in motion. Can you
tell us about that?

Dagmar: I had done a Tyrian workshop on Kelleys
Island called "The Mystery of the Blue Rose."
After that workshop, first one woman and
then a second Methodist woman came up to
me and asked if I'd be interested in pastoring
their church on the Island! I said, "I'm
Catholic." And they said, "We don't care!" I'd
been to a Methodist seminary. The woman
who had been the pastor was in the process of
retiring. They wanted to know if I'd be
interested.

Parker: In other words, they were suggesting you had
a "call."

Dagmar: Right. That was my first real, out-there, call.
First this one woman said it; then this other
woman came unrelated to the first woman
and said the same thing. They both belong to
the same church. Maybe they talked to each
other, but they weren't saying it together to
me.

When I got back to Cleveland, I called my
spiritual director and we sat down and I
started a discernment process as to whether or

not to take some extra courses, or whatever. To figure out what I would have to do to be ordained a Methodist minister.

In that discernment process, she pointed out quite rightly, if I did that I would de facto excommunicate myself. On reflection, it became pretty clear to me that while that was a "call," I was not interested in risking excommunication from my own denomination. Because I really didn't feel like I was going to be a good Methodist… I don't know, I didn't feel I had roots there.

I had connections there. I clearly had done some of my studying in their midst, but I didn't feel I was rooted there.

Parker: But you did know about it because your husband was Methodist, right?

Dagmar: I had no clue what a Methodist was about until I met him. I actually did my master's in theology and addiction counseling at a Methodist school while I was First Lady. I chose to go to a Methodist school, rather than the Josephinum which was a pontifical school, because they happened to have a master's program that included a degree in addiction counseling as part of their theological training. In fact, your professor was there at the time. Sharon.

Parker: Sharon Ringe? Oh, yes, she is now at Wesley
             Theological Seminary in Washington, D.C.
             An outstanding biblical scholar and
             translator.[11]

Dagmar: I thought about it carefully. I made a couple
             of calls to former students to find out what's
             involved. Everybody I talked to, a Lutheran
             friend and a Presbyterian friend and other
             Methodists, basically said, "You wouldn't be
             happy. It's still very hierarchical. The
             Methodist bishop pretty much tells you where
             you are going to go. There's no guarantee
             you'd ever land on the Island!" (laughter)

             That was the practicality of it. Basically, I'm
             just not a Protestant.

Parker: You know that the Methodists are a break-off
             from the Anglican church. So they retain that
             hierarchy.

"SOMETHING HAPPENED IN AUSTRIA"

Dagmar:

Right. So I decided, okay, this was a call but it wasn't a call to ordination in that sense. I thought I had put that to rest. But you bury stuff alive, and it has a way of resurrecting. So when the phone call came from Austria, Christine (Mayr-Lumetzberger) ... actually, I called her Evelyn or somebody had said, "Do you know the women are in the process of becoming ordained? They found bishops that will ordain them!" And I thought: Wonderful!

The first time I met Christine years ago, she told me that she was convinced that once these women went through their formation process, there would be a bishop there who would ordain them. I thought: She is talking through her head! She doesn't know what she is talking about! Not in our lifetime!

She told me there would be bishops. I heard it but I didn't believe it. Whenever I went back to Austria, I'd make a point of catching up with one or another of these women who were in formation

When I heard they had actually found bishops who were going to ordain them, I was very happy for them. I picked up the phone and I called Christine to congratulate her. Her response to me was, "Aren't you coming?"

I said I'd probably be there, I'd love to see you get ordained. She said, "No. Aren't *you* coming?" I *heard it*. Because I had been through this other process with the Methodist women. I said, "Christine, are you asking me whether you want me to be ordained with you?" She said, "Absolutely." I said, "What kind of bishops do you have?" I had just done this whole processing thing, and I wasn't going to get myself excommunicated over this.

She said: "With Roman Catholic bishops!" I heard myself saying, "If there are Roman Catholic bishops, I'll consider it." When I hung up, I thought to myself: *What are you talking about?* It was like I hadn't even spoken for myself.

Then we went through a whole discernment process, Evelyn and I together. I'll let Evelyn tell you a little bit about that. But at the tail-end of this, when I finally got to Austria and I met the bishops I realized, yeah, they were Roman Catholic bishops.

They were *married*.

If I had known this from the very beginning, it would have scared me off. But after all the stuff that I had been through up until then, I realized that this whole issue of who has what apostolic succession rites, how they got them, and how they didn't get them, and what is the difference between *valid and illicit*. And are

47

these bishops good enough for me?! What I heard was this internal voice saying: *they are good enough for you.*

"You are not good enough for anybody out there! This is not about official church. *This is who I can find willing to ordain women.* You're good enough, they're good enough: trust me!"

It was a process. All of us, even the most liberal among us, are still so convinced that this Roman Catholic church has it over everybody else. Somehow or other, there is nothing else that is valid. But if we cross all the "T's" and dot all the "I's", and do it the way the boys have designed how to do it, somehow it's not going to count.

Parker: Who's the bishop who actually ordained you?

Dagmar: There were two. Romulo Braschi was the one from Argentina. He is married.

Parker: He'd been excommunicated himself, hadn't he?

Dagmar: No. They say. He is excommunicated as much as any other married priest. I guess the difference is he's a married bishop. He may be de facto excommunicated. He's got a charismatic community that he worships with. I suppose married priests who choose to continue to read mass are de facto excommunicated, too. But that doesn't make the priesthood any less valid. It didn't make his bishophood any less valid.

The other one is somebody called Regelsberger. He's an Austrian.

Then there was a third bishop, who was one of the Czech underground bishops, who had been ordained by the bishop who had ordained Ludmila Javorova.[12] But as we discovered later on, he *had* come to Austria and had done the deacon ordinations. He said he was going to come back and participate in the priest ordinations. He didn't make it back in time. It was because supposedly one of the Franciscan communities that he was staying with discovered his intent, and they basically locked him up!

Roberta:	Oh! (gasp)
Parker:	You hadn't heard about that Roberta?
Roberta:	No, I hadn't.
Dagmar:	Yeah.
Evelyn:	I don't know about the intent part, but I did hear that from Christine. Maybe you could tell a bit more about the bishops who ordained you.
Dagmar:	The Austrian one is the one I connected with. Obviously. He's a very down-to-earth man

who was a Benedictine monk for about 20 or 30 years, and went to the missions in Brazil. Just like Braschi. Braschi was arrested by the Argentine dictators and then deserted by the church because the church was on the side of the dictators.

Regelsberger experienced Brazil -- which has a real need for priests and where women have been given all kinds of responsibilities, as way to keep the communities going. When he went to Brazil, he had a sabbatical from his Benedictine order. He fell in love with a Brazilian woman and married. He has a son in Brazil. The woman went away at some point or another with another man. He came back to Austria.

I spent a whole day with him. He took me to the community, one of the biggest Benedictine monasteries in Austria [Kremsmünster]. We had a wonderful day. I knew that this was the "testing" day.

I had put together this elaborate documentation, to prove that I might be worthy of this. Even though I went through this discernment process, at the end of it I did not make a decision: but decided to let these bishops decide. I figured I was putting together whatever documentation I could. I had the alb. I was preparing myself to be a priest, but I wasn't really sure that was going to happen.

When I got to Austria, my bag had not
followed me. In fact, my bag never arrived. I
had no alb, no documentation and figured:
O.K., that's it. That's a sign from God I'm not
supposed to do this. I called Christine and
said, "Christine, I have *nothing*. Not even a
second set of clothes to wear." She said, "So?
Come anyway."

I had a rental car and drove myself to this
place. Steinbach, Austria. Regelsberger spent
the day with me. At the end of that he said,
"We don't need any documentation." That
was pretty much what I was also picking up.
My head said: This is a sign of God. You lost
your documentation, you've lost your
vestments, you're obviously not supposed to
do this.

But inside it was: .Uh, Uh, You are not going
to get off that easy.' (laughter)

Evelyn: And I was supposed to be there with
               your stole!

Dagmar: Evelyn never made it either. She was supposed
               to use it in the investiture. It was like every
               day something happened. The minute I had a
               doubt, something happened that (slapping her
               hands together) made it disappear. I was never
               saying: Well, if you really want me to do this,
               show me something that makes it clear. I
               wasn't that obnoxious. But there were times

51

when I thought: This just makes no sense. What are you supposed to do with this? Look at these bishops; they're not even real bishops.

But *I was doing it* even though they were not "real" bishops. Whatever they were. It was clear that it was going to be *illicit.*

I had no idea where they were going to do the ordination. There were all these churches around us, and I'd pick another church to go to mass in the morning. I was thinking, are we going to do it here? Where are they going to do it? The fire station? Where is this going to happen? 'Cause everything was kept secret. They didn't want the press to know. These people kept the Franciscan bishop locked up…they would have kept, who knows?

The day before the ordination, that evening, the superior of the Benedictine order came in person to the house and sat down with Regelsberger. I was sitting in the room. He looked at me and said, "This is going to be a private conversation, so you had better leave." Regelsberger looked at me, and looked at him and said, "She can stay." (groans)

The superior was furious. He just lit into this guy: "It was bad enough that you didn't come back from the sabbatical, and that you got married, and look what God did to you— took your woman away because you didn't deserve her … , and your son is in Brazil and you don't deserve him…. Instead of being repentant, you just …. You will …."

It was just the most horrible, scary, frightening, disgusting thing! I was so enraged. At one point, I just lit into him. He was this…monsignor, or whatever the hell he was. I said, "I think you have said enough. Could you just leave? We need to prepare for tomorrow. This is just a lot of bad energy you are bringing to this house." Regelsberger was just kind of smiling. He said, "That's O.K. Let him vent." It was just horrible. Then he left.

But some of the other women who had been ordained deacons ended up not doing it. Because they were so terrorized by their parish priests, by various people in their families. The day we got the vestments, that were sowed by a Lutheran woman, we took one set of vestments to this one woman who had been ordained a deacon, who was also a religion teacher. For forty years she had been a religion teacher. She couldn't get out of bed, she was so afraid. Because people had so lit into her. We walked in and we gave her the vestments. She put them on. I can never forget this, she stood in front of the mirror, with just tears pouring down her face. "I can't do it, I can't do it. It is just too hard! This is how far I'm going to get in my lifetime. But thank you."

THE DISCERNMENT PROCESS IN THE AMERICAN HINTERLAND

Parker: Dagmar, you prepared yourself by going on retreat previous to going to Austria, after you decided to be open to this call. Can you and Ev describe that?

Evelyn: I think it was Dagmar who found a setting in the countryside in spirit with a discernment process.

Parker: On the timing: the Austrian call (with Christine) was in February 2002. When did you go on retreat?

Dagmar: In May? In between that period of time I spent some time with my spiritual director talking it over. Who pretty much said, "You are still going to be excommunicated." I said, "Yes, but this is different. This is now Roman Catholic bishops. I suppose they will be excommunicated with us." This is a step in the direction that we need to take. I had put together a discernment circle of different people that I was talking to. Some priests. And of course, my family. Everybody, but one, was very supportive. That was Martha Church. That was going on before I went to the retreat, but I had set the date for the retreat.

Parker: Did you consult with your confessor? I don't know quite how this protocol works.

Dagmar:	No. On advice from my spiritual director I did not raise it with my confessor.
Parker:	Ev, you were talking about the retreat?
Evelyn:	This was set after Dagmar had done some discernment. This was towards the end of that…. Dagmar decided to set up the sequence of the retreat based on the seven sacraments.
Dagmar:	And based on the formation process that Christine Lumetzberger had done with the other women except that they had spent three years doing it. And I was spending ten days doing it. The formation process was based on the sacraments. We said one sacrament a day.
Parker:	Okay, you start with baptism. What else did you do?
Evelyn:	We did spend two days on penance. (laughter)
Dagmar:	I got Martha Church (pseudonym) that day. Such a gift. (murmurs)
Parker:	Tell us about that.
Dagmar:	I had invited her into my first discernment circle, because she is a national leader and also a member of a group of women who feel called to ordination. But they were just meeting twice a year, trying to stay in

conversation with a few bishops. So I decided … well, Roberta, you were there….

Parker: What happened? We are going to run out the tape in about five minutes.

Dagmar: Martha listened carefully, then asked a couple of questions. At the end of my first conversation with her, she told me she thought I should forward all of the articles written about me in the *Plain Dealer* to the bishops in Austria. I said I wouldn't give the *Plain Dealer* that kind of credibility; they are going to get my book.[13] That would suffice. That would give them all the bad things I have done.

She seemed very supportive in many ways. At one point, she burst into tears, and said, "There is no question you have a genuine call. But maybe you should wait a couple of years and take a few more courses." But what she did, unbeknownst to me, is that *she* chose to copy all the different articles in the *Plain Dealer,* and shipped them with a cover letter to Austria, saying that she didn't think I was qualified. She said Catholics would not accept this; and that this was going to be a detriment to women's ordination down the road. And, and, and…

When Christine Lumetzberger got that, Christine went with her own perceptions of my call, and saved all of that stuff until I got there. When I got there, she handed it to me and said, "You can burn it, or you can give it back to her, or you can put it in your archives, but it is no good to us. This is not how we make decisions. Here we call this 'mobbing,' when somebody goes after somebody that way." (murmurs)

She wrote this to me in an email. I had no idea Martha had done this. So the day I was in discernment on retreat, dealing with the sacrament of penance, I got this email from Christine Lumetzberger saying she had a box full of copies of articles we're not even going to go through but she saw the cover letter. "I just want you to know what is happening. You may want to stop talking to this person for awhile."

Dagmar: I sat with Evelyn and some others. Someone finally said, "The best thing to do is to let it go." But that took a day! (laughter)

Parker: Tell me about the day as you saw it, Ev.

Evelyn: I remember we were trying to plug the damn computer in! (laughter) To figure out this email, and get a table to put it on. It was sort of like rolling thunder. You had something, you had an email from her previous to that where you were back and forth with her. It was like it kept getting worse and worse. And we were hanging on tenterhooks with whatever was going to be coming forth in this

57

email. I mean it was a struggle. It was a real struggle.

Dagmar: I composed a reply to Martha, but didn't actually send it. Maybe by accident I sent it to a few people, because I didn't know what I was doing on the computer. And I started getting replies back, "what's going on here." It was a mess.

That was never the issue, to stop the retreat. But it was a time to *forgive* right on the spot! It came right on the day of the sacrament of penance. I suppose it was the whole intent, if there is a higher power intent, there. She certainly didn't derail my ordination. In fact, she was the one who told me at one point, "If it's God's will, nothing can stop it. And if it isn't, nothing can help it." You know, she was right.

Evelyn: I just think it was such a challenging time. Because we were all trying to figure out what the spirit was saying in all of this. That was the challenge. *It was just like the activity of God was right there in all these conversations.* That's what I thought. Truly the spirit of God was working in ways that were challenging in everyone at the same time.

Parker: God didn't let up a bit.

Dagmar: And we had to move on, to the sacrament of eucharist, and celebrating our first eucharist.

There was no way of doing that until I put that behind. In a way, in retrospect, it makes perfect sense. At the time, it was …

Parker: What is your take on this, Roberta?

Roberta: Dagmar asked me to come to that dinner, because I happened to be free that night. I'm glad I went though, because I was a witness to this woman. I had not known her. I didn't know who she was…. I didn't catch on that there was anything behind this until … We had had this pleasant meeting and dinner.

When Dagmar showed me this email, I thought: unbelievable. And we both talked about "it's only a woman who is going to do this thing to you." But what she fell right back into was the whole bureaucracy of the church-already: "She's not qualified. You're not the person we need to send out there. You are not qualified."

How bureaucratic, how *male* can you get? Instead of saying, let's go back to our discernment and yes, support her: she went off on this awful thing.

Parker: Was she operating from fear?

Roberta: Fear and jealousy.

Dagmar: She, herself, at one point had a call to ordination. She says right now she doesn't want to be ordained in this kind of bureaucracy. But, she's become the bureaucracy!

What's interesting is yesterday I went to a fundraiser, and a friend of Martha's came up to me and said, "I fully expect to be ordained in my lifetime. I've had a call for years. I want you to know I have no intention of doing a Master's in Divinity in order to do so." (laughter)

I said, "Whatever! Whatever floats your boat. We need all kinds of people, including maybe Master's in Divinity, I happen to have a Master's in Counseling and some theology." And she said, "Oh, I cannot believe that Martha would insist on that kind of academic qualification, because we need a completely different open process from what we've ever had …." In a way Martha has exposed herself ,and I'm sure she's getting some advice, some insight, we had her at lunch….

Evelyn: Yes, we had her for lunch at the local WOC meeting.

Dagmar: The local WOC group doesn't know what side to take.

Roberta: They're still talking about "sides" here. They shouldn't have sides.

Dagmar: They gave me a stole.

Evelyn: Remember, we were invited to talk about the
                 Dublin conference at the local WOC meeting.

EXCOMMUNICATION

Parker: So you came back from the Danube ordained. What has been your reception? You have been excommunicated officially. That's on appeal?

Dagmar: Right. I've discovered there are two kinds of excommunication. There is de facto excommunication, which you incur if you do some horrible thing according to the church, like remarry without annulment, have an abortion, etc. And then there is this particular excommunication, "reserved to the Holy See." The local bishop can't undo it.

If I wanted to recant, I would have to apply to Rome. Ratzinger personally would have to grant it (then head of the Congregation for the Defense of the Faith, the future Pope Benedict XVI), or the pope, I don't know. The reality is had they not excommunicated us, it would have been worse. See if I had just gone and become an ordained minister in the Methodist church, Ratzinger would not have paid any attention. De facto excommunication, you do it to yourself, they don't care. It won't make a dent.

But with us, they had a cardinal, Ratzinger, excommunicate us, with no recourse through the local bishops.[14] So you know that something has gotten under their skin.

Furthermore, everybody's talking about it, again.

We didn't know how to move this baby along. Now it's moving again. I said to the woman at the fundraiser: "You want to be ordained, get ordained! There are bishops willing to ordain you. They may not be *licit* but they are *valid*. We need all kinds of women to step forward. There needs to be wave after wave of women getting ordained." I said the same thing to the two women at church today: "Do you want to make a difference? Get yourself ordained." Their priest a couple of months ago took all of his Roman collars, and went from pew to pew, and handed Roman collars to people in his congregation.

Evelyn:	Wow.
Dagmar:	He handed one to a woman for work she's been doing on hospitality, and one to this woman for work she's been doing as a reader... He said, "I'm not wearing them anymore. You are the priests." (murmurs)

This is all unbeknownst to me. So when I got the Roman collar, I thought: Let's find somebody to give this to. It is happening. Every time I think: "Am I just too much full of myself? Is this just a figment of my imagination?" Something like this happens that I could have no way predicted or planned or have done anything about, to confirm that

63

	we are all in this together. We are all on the path of the spiritual warriors! (laughter)
Parker:	Back to spiritual warriors! In practical terms, you can't go back "home again" anymore, can you?
Dagmar:	Actually, I can. They were told that the rule is that they cannot let me come to mass. I called the vicar for religious, myself, told her that we have an appeal in. My understanding is that until Ratzinger is willing to hear the appeal, the punishment does not stand. She acknowledged that she was told to call these communities, she didn't want to. She has to do what she has to do.

[end of tape 1]

THE "STEELING" TIME

Parker: Let's resume. Evelyn, why don't you go ahead.

Evelyn: We were going to talk about the discernment
             retreat, which was about in the middle of
             May, 2002. I can't imagine that it is still in the
             same year. Amazing. It has been a year of
             mystery and for the spirit dwelling
             everywhere.

             One of the things that we wanted to do was to
             go through the seven sacraments in ways that
             discern what the essence of the sacrament was,
             what it meant in the life of a person who was
             a Catholic, especially someone called to
             ordination. It was a ten-day retreat, although
             we both took off for two days in the middle to
             take care of other things.

             We wanted a horarium of some kind, which is
             a daily schedule. We wanted to do the prayers
             of the divine hours. We had some wonderful
             readings, a book of those. We decided we
             would do readings from that at different times
             during the day.... Dagmar decided, "Oh, I
             guess I have to put this together myself.
             Discern the direction I want to go in, and
             how I am to do this."

             So I found it very enlightening even, to be
             with her. She would ask questions along the
             way, which I thought were good.

Dagmar: By virtue of having Evelyn there, it became much more of a communal process…

Evelyn: That was very good…. We were there, were trying to think through the process, what was coming down the road, and Dagmar hadn't decided at this point whether to be ordained, and how this was going to work out. It was very intense. All of us were trying to figure out, what do you do in a church like this that is preventing you as a female from having the gift of priesthood, from having access to one of the sacraments, one of the seven sacraments? As one of the German women said in one of her writings, we have seven sacraments, but women have only access to six. *Baptism* is supposed to be the doorway to the sacraments. We were all struggling with this whole part about the Catholic church.

One day we walked down to a lake. It was very nice and spring-like. We decided to read through the baptismal rite, which is a special sacramentary book.

We went down to the lake, and we used sprigs of flowering crabapple, and blessed each other with the water, like we were doing a baptism. We did that rite down by the lake. It was wonderful. It brought me back to the life of Jesus, in a sense of doing something in a natural setting with a person who is a believer, with the water there… It is very much *out* of the institution, out of a church building, and in a natural setting, like it seemed to be intended to.

Parker: You mentioned off-tape that it was like first-century Christendom.

Evelyn: It would be like we'd be back following the footsteps of Jesus, with some of his disciples, apostles, doing things right then, without this huge structure of hierarchy, without a lot of formality...

Dagmar: Lydia...

Evelyn: That's right, following the footsteps of Lydia who had an early house-church, a leader in the Pauline community.

Parker: She was a merchant who sold dye?

Dagmar: Yes, Tyrian dye!

Evelyn: Purple dye.

Dagmar: She would meet the women at the water's edge. That is where Paul met her.

Evelyn: That was rather inspiring, to do that. And all the while we were doing this, we were also thinking eventually of going through the mass, sort of a practice run. We were collecting things that would be symbolic for that.

Parker: Which day was this?

Dagmar: We spent one day on baptism, two days on
               penance, the next day eucharist. It was the
               fourth day.

Evelyn: We were gathering symbols and artifacts that
               were meaningful, to bring part of ourselves
               into the celebration.

Dagmar: We had to go buy wine, of course. We didn't
               have it yet.

Evelyn: Right. So we made a foray out to a little
               convenient-mart, a little rural place actually,
               with a few truckers around, and some neon
               signs advertising the lottery. (laughter) We
               tried to figure out if we were going to buy this
               $5 wine. (laughter) We did go in there and
               bought a bottle of wine, and took a picture
               out in front, with Dagmar holding the wine
               bottle. Was there something else we were
               getting?

Dagmar: A butterfly. We wanted to have a butterfly on
               the altar. One of those plastic things that they
               were selling. I had brought a piece of cloth
               that you had given me, Evelyn. I don't know
               where you bought that.

Evelyn: In Ireland… It had purple coloring in it and
               spirals…

Dagmar:	We set up a make-shift altar for the eucharistic celebration. So we put this cloth on it, I brought some candles. I had painted a stone with a purple heart on it. (*See* photo of replica, p. 104)
Evelyn:	I made a cross. It had a little saying on it, out of Philip Newell's book, a poem. We brought some shells. We brought some twigs from down by the lake. We got some flowers from the fields, and some iris. Very feminist things, I think. I had a little sign that said 'cornerstone'. We put this in front of the lectern.
Parker:	Then you go through a mass, a practice mass.
Evelyn:	Yes; we have the mass book. We tried to do this in our rooms. I remember trying to go through it. There were so many tabs on this book, ribbons and everything. It is a mystery, actually, how to do it. I think we had a missal there, too. I remember we were up there, trying to read the prayers. There were some directions, they were all printed in red.
	We seemed to be doing fine. We got to this one part, turning the page, and there was nothing connected to what we just did. I started laughing! What happens now? I commented: "this is what they teach you in seminary!"

Dagmar: The reading of the day – I had gone to mass
            that morning, and I could tell from the missal
            that we had – that Jesus was asking Peter three
            times, "Do you love me?" And Peter getting
            slightly vexed. "How many more times are
            you going to ask me?"

            Then we did a dialogue about it. Me trying to
            preach on it. Me having a conversation about
            what we thought it meant. What was
            interesting about this was that the ordination
            on the Danube was on the Feast Day of Peter
            and Paul, which seems to be the classic
            ordination day in the Catholic church, at least
            in Europe. The women who had planned the
            ordination had put together a missal and a
            program. They wanted the bishops to use the
            portion from scripture where Jesus appears to
            Mary Magdalene after the resurrection. But
            the Argentinian bishop insisted upon using
            the reading for the day – which happened to
            be the reading we had practiced on. So from
            my perspective, it was perfect. (laughter)

Parker: The practice mass. Tell me more.

Evelyn: The mass book does have directions on every
            page, when to do the prayer, what follows…

Dagmar: And what gestures. Everything. Whether or
            not to breathe at the right time.

Evelyn: It made me think, that these young priests
            who come out of the seminary, the men, have

this in front of them all the time, so it is not that mysterious. It looks mysterious when you don't see the book. But with all the directions there, it is not that mysterious. I ended up doing the reading of the directions. And Dagmar would say the prayer.

Dagmar: We were like co-celebrating. But, I have to say, preparing for this, then actually going through with it was like *breaking through a taboo.* Especially, as you got to the actual words of consecration, you sort of imagine that the sky will open and all hell will break loose. Of course, none of that happened, it was wonderful. It was just fine, thank you. But breaking through these taboos is not simple.

Evelyn: There is something out there that is so mysterious that you can't understand it, can't participate. That's the way it has been, women haven't been able to participate. It has been very mysterious to most women. It's almost like, this is what needs to happen. Women need to walk through that door, even though it has been closed to us. To use the ability that God has graced us with.

Parker: Where did you get the consecrated wafer?

Evelyn: I don't know if they were consecrated. But we did get wafers.

Roberta: It could be anything, even a piece of toast.

Evelyn: But this was practice.

Dagmar: It was practice, but it was also my first mass.

Evelyn: We got the wine. It was perfect. No one else
              was around. We basically did this on our own.
              And were very reverent about all of it. I think
              what I wanted to do, certainly to be there as a
              companion, but experience the prayer as if it
              were something going on in seminary, the
              training for ordination kind of thing.

Dagmar: I did the sacrament earlier at mass in a village
              church. I went to confession.

              Then Evelyn had to get back to Cleveland for
              a couple of days. I had to go to Columbus to
              be present for a friend who was graduating. As
              it happened she was graduating from Capital
              University, which was a university where I had
              taken my first theological class; they have a
              Lutheran school there. I had graduated myself
              from Capital University. So in my mind it was
              part of the confirmation.

              I had found a volume of Susan Bollens'
              paintings. There was a beautiful painting in it.
              And we used this ritual...

Evelyn: Which was called "to embrace paradox" – how
              to carry on for justice in the face of injustice,
              to celebrate the power of women. We had the
              prayers, they were Native American prayers.
              We did that. We tried to bring things together

from our own experience, to make it very concrete. There was another book with a couple of prayers in them that were very relevant. I read from them. I read one of them during the mass that we were doing; and I read one a little later.

Dagmar: The next day, the next sacrament was last rites. We decided to pay our respects to Marilyn Theotokos (pseudonym), a dear friend, as a symbol of all those who risk greatly and die at the height of their powers.

Evelyn: We remembered some of her writings. We remembered her life. We talked about some of the ways we knew her, some of the ways I knew her and had been with her. We prayed for her, standing in the grain of the fields. I recalled her funeral, I was in the funeral. I had written a poem about that, too.

Parker: Would Marilyn have approved of all this?

Evelyn/Dagmar: Oh, yes. (in unison)

Dagmar: We told her at the grave, "Look what you've gotten us into!" That was another one who died, left us holding the bag.

Evelyn: I knew Marilyn was definitely for women's ordination. First of all, we were good friends. Years before, Jane Bunyan (pseudonym), one of our mutual friends, had died in an auto crash. Marilyn and I had gone to the funeral in Atlanta. Jane was from an Irish family. And the family was beside themselves: she had become an Episcopalian. She wasn't a priest; she was a retreat director.

They had a funeral there. But it was like high-church, Episcopal. But her family wanted us to do the rosary at the prayer service beforehand. We decided, instead of using the usual mysteries of the rosary, three sets of mysteries – we decided to make up sets of our own. Myself, and a friend, Rebecca, and Marilyn. We were the ones who did the readings of the rosary. Jane would have loved it. There were Rebecca and Marilyn and I, we made these up on the spot. It was very feminist. I'm sure the people in the chapel were totally shocked. But we just knew that it was the right thing to do at her funeral. Definitely from that, I knew that Marilyn was right there....

Parker: And we know that Dagmar, early, learned to think for herself under a canon lawyer in Trieste, Lotte Leitmeyer.

Dagmar: Yes. She was definitely there, too.

Evelyn: It's like walking in the footsteps of these other women.

ORDINATION ON THE DANUBE

Dagmar: The fact was the "call" came from Austria and, as it unfolded, the ordination was on the Danube. I was born on the Danube, I was married on the Danube. Before I was ordained, the last email I got that day was from Dick who basically wrote, "I know how seriously you take vows taken on the bank of the Danube. I wish you well." Christine Mayr-Lumetzberger said, "We'll be doing this on a boat We'll be going from Passau toward Linz. We won't know where we are going to be ordained, in Germany or Austria." If I had tried to design it for myself, it couldn't have been more appropriate.

It turned out I was the only one who could speak to the Argentinian bishop. Because he only spoke Spanish, Italian, and of course, Latin. But he didn't speak much German. I spent a lot of time talking with him in Italian. He brought in a band of native Indian/Peruvian musicians. He insisted on that. The German and Austrian women were saying, "We have our own plans." For me it was perfect, because it was some sense of the Americas, present. The music wasn't just Gregorian chants or folk music or Austrian songs. It was these Native American musicians.

We took off. I had to be ordained deacon before the priestly ordination. They took me

75

upstairs for that. Evelyn was supposed to be there and do the investiture. She wasn't there. But my son Christopher was there with his three kids. And so my oldest granddaughter, Eleanor, ended up putting on the vestment.

They laid on hands: first, in the Roman ritual the Roman bishop laid on hands, then the Lutheran representative laid on hands, and then the Anglican representative laid on hands, and then the Old Catholic Utrecht representative laid on hands, and the Old Catholic from Italy laid on hands. They all brought gifts.

The Catholics gave us the oils to use in last rites; the Lutherans gave us a written thing; and the Italians gave us some aprons for service – the Italian talked about the importance of the priest for service. The apron had alpine flowers; these were Italians from northern Italy, and edelweiss; and embroidered upon it, the motto of the State of Ohio! With God all things are possible! In German. (laughter)

As we were being ordained, there was this crunching, this horrible noise on the boat. It felt like we were stuck. And we were! In a lock. A murmur went through the crowd, "O my God." As these two bishops were laying on hands, the locks opened! And we just moved through peacefully.

The press representatives that were on the boat wanted to get off the boat as quickly as possible to file their stories. They had made arrangements to dock the boat right after the ordination. But the captain made a mistake, and ended up docking on the wrong side of the river. (laughter) The reporters were let go, but there were no phones for them. There they were! (laughter) [15]

On the left side there, as we were approaching the dock, was a giant pile of wood, like for burning witches! In Austria they make these big fires along the Danube for celebrating the summer solstice. This was not just the Feast of Peter and Paul, but also the eve of the summer solstice. June 29, 2002. Everyone was making jokes about the fate of these ordained women.

But we made it through the lock, and past the burning pile, and the reporters were gone. And had this big feast. By then my grandchildren were asleep, especially Julia, really the one who helped me make the final decision. When I told her mom that I was thinking about getting ordained, the conversation with Melanie -- being a doctor -- was very practical: "what do you know about saying a mass? What do you know about...?"

I said, "I know nothing; those are things I can learn." Julia pipes up, she's on her mom's lap: "So, Dagmar, you want to be a priest?" I said, "I'm thinking about it, honey." Julia's response: "Cool! That means I can be a priest!"

That sort of clinched it for me. There were all these other things. Friends, and family, the sermon, da-da-da... Ultimately, I looked at my own granddaughter and thought, Hey, if I do nothing but get it through their head it is possible – that will do!

Parker: How old was she at the time?

Dagmar: Eight. Earlier, when we were driving toward Passau with my grandson Max in the car, he asked: "Are you the first American woman priest?... Wow, you mean I can tell my friends in school, my grandmother..." It was this combination of very serious and almost spooky kind of stuff. And then this totally natural, normal thing...

You know, there is *nothing more natural* than for a woman standing at the altar and saying, "This is *my* body, this is my *blood.*" Because we do it. *It is. It is not defiling.* It is what it is. When women talk about *feeding with their own substance*, we know what we are talking about. We've been there.

Parker: You're defining your theology of call from a feminist point of view. It is giving your body and blood.

Dagmar: Right. It is the very reason that they say "is why we cannot do it." It is, in fact, because it is the most ... *natural,* instead of whatever they've invented.

THE DANUBE 7

Parker: Dagmar, would you mind telling me about the others, beginning with Ida Raming?

Dagmar: What do you want to know?

Parker: A little bit about them. For most of us, we'd have to go look it up, in German!

Dagmar: Ida Raming is a theologian. She has been working on women's ordination for about forty years. She presented an official letter to Vatican II, asking them to discuss women's ordination – which of course did not happen.

Her partner, maybe friend, certainly, Iris Müller is a theologian. But she is very ill. Under the circumstances, I think they would never have ordained her. I think this is why Ida decided 'it was now, or never'. Iris was working in a university library, and put together a feminist collection of theology there.

Parker: Gisela Forster?

Dagmar: Gisela Forster, I don't know a lot about Gisela, except she is the person who organized the German piece[16] of this. Gisela is married, she's got kids, she is I think a teacher, like Christine.

80

Christine Mayr-Lumetzberger was a former sister. She is married to Michael Mayr. She teaches handicapped children. She's the one who pretty much invented the formation process for the women. Pretty much, with Gisela, organized the whole thing.

Adelaide Roitinger is a sister of a teaching order. She has been teaching for thirty, forty years. I don't know what happened to her, whether she is still in the order.

I know zero about Pia Roma. I think she just came. I think she was also operating under a different name. That may or may not be her real name. But the thing about her is that she is actually a Lutheran. I guess it was a conversion experience of sorts. Or she didn't think that being ordained in the Lutheran church was where she wanted to be. I didn't have much of a chance to get to know her.

Roberta: Is that all of them? (nod)

Evelyn: So they are all different. All these different backgrounds, countries…

Dagmar: And as I said, there were a couple more who were ordained deacons, but didn't continue.

Parker: These six women went through a three-year preparation for ministry? Designed their own curriculum?

Dagmar: Christine designed the curriculum. Gisela, Adelaide, and Iris, Pia (I'm not sure).

THE COMPANIONS OF CONSCIENCE

Parker: Dagmar's gone through the intellectual process. I'm wondering also about the feeling stage, the ups and downs. What is your take of the process she went through?

Roberta: I was most appreciative of the process she went through. Probably, at the time, it might have produced more fear than I thought. She was so into the process, the method, the discernment, to make a retreat, she was really deciding this for the incredible life decision it was. When she had doubts, we would talk about it, and with Evelyn, and her spiritual advisor. I am just in awe of how it all happened. I don't believe I contributed that much, except to listen. I probably didn't appreciate how difficult it really was.

Dagmar: Let me say this. I think having Evelyn and Roberta as close by, and as available, the most important thing to me was it helped me stay on this side of sanity. In the sense that, if she had said, "Hey, you are really off the deep end!" I would have had to take that seriously.

Parker: In other words, she was a source of affirmation

Dagmar: Affirmation. But also I needed confirmation that this was a doable, sane...

Evelyn: And genuine...

Dagmar: thing.

Dagmar: I implicitly trusted each of these people. I
                think they would have told me if they thought
                I was just nuts….

                I'm also grateful to my spiritual adviser, very
                much into labyrinths. The process of walking
                the labyrinth helps you clarify the question.
                Maybe receive some kind of insight.

                So before going to walk the labyrinth, I said,
                "What do you think I should ask?" The
                response: "It is your walk." I insisted: "It is *my*
                walk, but it is also *our* church. What kind of
                question should I ask?" Eventually, my
                spiritual adviser suggested: "How about a very
                Zen question? Why don't you ask yourself:
                What is the Path, with What?" It took me
                back to 'it is only with the heart that we can
                see right'.

                I found a labyrinth during the discernment
                retreat. As I was walking through, I had all the
                experiences of my life that were heart-
                warming experiences, and all kinds of
                experiences that just came at me. When I
                stepped into the center of the labyrinth, there
                is this rose. It is a six-fold rose. There was a
                rock in the middle of it. And (clearing the frog
                in her throat), I remember thinking the thing
                I hadn't thought of yet. All my children. All

six of them. There they were. I thought of them child-by-child.

And then, I didn't know whether to step on that rock, around that rock, the little symbol of Peter – right there in the middle. On the way out, I had the answer that I was looking for. It wasn't *my* decision about ordination. The bishops were going to make this decision. The path, the part, for me was to walk as far as I could walk, and do the process as well as I could do. And to leave the result to the bishops.

The retreat, on the one hand, was confirming a lot of things, breaking some of the taboos. But basically, I walked out the way I walked in. Not decided. A bit wiser, but not decided. I continue to ask that question. What is the path with heart, here.

It is ultimately, I can't operate with just anger at the injustice of it all. I have to operate from a place of compassion, a place of love, for this very sick church. Otherwise, why be a priest in this church?

Evelyn: I think of it as grace. I know it is a big Catholic term and we have all heard of it in our classes. But for me, each step in that retreat, each of those is a grace. The gift of God, somehow. Persons that appear to you, and say things that connect you to your history is a grace.

Dagmar: Even Martha Church – her opposition, in
               good conscience -- came at the right point in
               that retreat. It forced me to stretch beyond
               what I thought I wanted to do in terms of
               forgiveness.

Evelyn: It was perfect timing. (murmurs)

Dagmar: I later told her: "You played a significant piece
               in this! It was an obstacle to overcome.!"

Parker: Let me push you on this, on the sacrament of
               penance. You had to forgive her, right? You
               had to forgive this crazy church, and whatever
               they were going to do. Because you have to let
               God be God. Do it for him, or her. And you
               had to forgive Dick?

Dagmar: Oh, Dick wasn't even an issue. I mean, what
               happened with Dick in this was kind of like a
               byproduct. It became very clear to me, that
               without the divorce, I would not have been
               able to follow through.

Parker: But it's in February. I am just going back to
               your statement that Ev showed me, to
               Christine in Austria. In February, that is when
               Dick remarried? Or is that when he had a
               child? I'm kind of …. And then your mother-
               in-law was dying. About three things were
               going on.

| Dagmar: | That was before. He got married about six months after the divorce. |

Dagmar: That was before. He got married about six months after the divorce.

Parker: What was happening in February 2002 when you got that call? (silence) Maybe I've just got this confused.

Dagmar: We had come to live in Cleveland.

Parker: It doesn't matter. Just what you had to do to be free, yourself, to be able to go on. That is what I was getting at. I guess the process was worked out partly through the sacrament of penance in the hinterland.

Dagmar: Ev, what does that do? In any other consecrated type of life, I would have had to annul my marriage. I don't believe my marriage is annullable. I am sure I could get it annulled, because the rules are so…, you pay your $2,000. But *I* don't think it is annullable. So I ended up with these married bishops, and divorced bishops! I had to let go of a lot of preconceived notions about what is right and wrong.

Roberta: That is the hardest part.

Dagmar: In accepting the bishops, I kind of let go of some of the final vestiges of judgment I was still holding against Dick for going through with the divorce. He is a Protestant anyway! From his standpoint, he didn't do anything that wasn't acceptable anyway. For me, it was a challenge; it is a challenge. I feel like ordination and marriage are compatible. But in my life, if I had remained married I would have been in India, playing wife of the ambassador… I wouldn't have been able to follow this. So if this is what God has in store for me, I'll be divorced. (laughter)

Parker: 21st century, marriage, divorce…

Dagmar: Plus, I have so much more empathy for people who have to go through this. Leaving a community, or leaving a spouse, or horrendous losses, with children or whatever. This experience is valuable in this sense.

Evelyn: God speaks to you through all of it. It is like Saint Theresa said, "Everything is a grace." In a way, what happens to you is God's way of getting your attention. God speaks to you through all of this.

Dagmar: One of the things that did happen with Dick. I asked him what he thought. He came over to my apartment for some reason. After we were discussing whatever we were discussing, maybe my book, I told him that I was going through this discernment process, and what did he think? I said, "And by the way, you were the first person who actually called me on this. At the time when you did it, I thought it was just uncalled for." I was offended.

Because he said to me at some point during one of the fights during the divorce, "I don't know why you are fighting this so much. You were never meant to be my wife. You were meant to be a priest." I thought, "What's this all about priests? Now there's an excuse." He went through all this rigamarole about being celibate without being celibate. I thought he was throwing at me all this stuff he had no business even using.

But I said to him, "You were the first person to call me on this. What was going on in your head?" He said, "I always believed that. I think that whether it is in my denomination, or in your denomination, I can't think of a better person to be a minister or a priest, than you." I said, "What I'd like you to do is pray with me and bless me." So he did. There was crying. I think it was a healing piece. Since then ... we've had much better conversations, he is interested in this whole thing. Very positive when the press calls him and asks him questions. We are in a different place that way.

Parker: Roberta, what did you want to add to this? You said, somewhere, there is a problem with the church. What were you onto? These various conflicts that Dagmar was facing.

Roberta: I don't remember what I was going to say. But the ability to make her decision and hand it to people she'd never met in the church bureaucracy, to put the decision in their

	hands, just boggles the mind. Holding that bureaucracy accountable, which it hasn't ever been for women, at the same time putting the decision in their hands, is just incredible.
Dagmar:	But that is just it. The Danube 7 bishops have been through the same thing, they have been rejected because they are married…
Roberta:	But that is not why you accepted them. It is because they are a part of the same church, able to make it happen to you…
Evelyn:	Through the apostolic succession.
Dagmar:	Yes, but the apostolic succession only matters in terms of fighting back to these people who say it is not licit. I say today to women, in every profession when 30% of the profession becomes female, the whole profession sinks. (laughter)
Roberta:	No, they just make more money. When it becomes 30% women? The 70%, the boys, keep the money.
Dagmar:	We buy into that if we say status is where it is at. When we look at the priests, they have to lose status in order for lay people to be in. In terms of ordination, we have to have more and more women irrespective of whether the ordinations are legitimate. We have to de-legitimize the 'high priest', to bring it down to a level where it can actually be equal…

Evelyn: And be pastoral.

Parker: The tipping point that has to be reached, before women can be part of the old boys' network, the leadership.

Dagmar: I don't want to be part of the old boys' network yet. It's not in order to be part of that, it is to go in there consciously, in order to bring them down. Because, they have to come down from their high-horse, to be able to become the priests and church that they need to be.

Roberta: They understand this very well.

Dagmar: They understand this very well and that is why they are fighting us.

Parker: Women as a group challenging their leadership.

Roberta: The medical profession, lawyers, name it.

Evelyn: They just are holding on, desperately, I think.

Parker: The women have made a difference, in some cases. Let's get to 'larger church'. You are coming back now as a priest. What kinds of situations are you facing, what is your relation to the crisis in the Catholic church?

Dagmar: The first situation I was facing was whether or not I could step into a Catholic church. And then, I am discovering that I am being invited. I am just going where I am invited. There was a point where I said, O.K. I'm going to break this rule in my own parish, because it is my pastor, my confessor. If he is going to kick me out, he is going to have to do it himself. I've got this sense, it's not about fighting any one person, even. Look, there is a church here, a priest there, a sister here, you are more than welcome. You don't have to accept their ballgame, at all.

Parker: They don't define you anymore.

Dagmar: They don't define me, they don't define the priesthood, they don't define the church. I will find the people I need to find to be priest with. And they can be priests to me, because they can bring me communion.

Parker: One person you mentioned, your confessor. I noticed in the *Plain Dealer* article that he said something about you. He was identified as your confessor.

Dagmar: No, he is not (identified).

Parker: Or did I just know that?

Dagmar: You knew that. He is identified as the chancellor.

The chancellor said I'm excommunicated, he also sent it to me in writing and a fairly cordial letter with it. I am not permitted to participate in ministerial activities or receive sacraments. For most people stepping inside a church, sitting in a pew is not participating in ministerial activities. But they can choose to interpret it that way if they want to give to the Vatican more power than they usually do. Just by virtue of being there, you are part of the Mass essential.

Parker: But isn't that dehumanizing? He is parroting the rules, but he may also have been your confessor. That is a different kind of relationship.

Dagmar: Yes. Except I didn't confess to him. He had no clue. I pretty much went to my spiritual director, who said "If you are going to go to him, he is going to do what he has to do." ....And that is true. But at the same time, from a human perspective he may have felt that I should have sat down with him before sitting down with the bishop. And told him something about it in person. (cell phone rings)

Parker: The crisis of the larger church? Do you two want to get into this while Dagmar talks?

Evelyn: I think the crisis in the larger church is pretty much addressed by the new book out, "The Sacred Silence." The whole crisis of authority of the bishops and what they have done. The sex scandal, the pedophilia scandal. I think there is a big crisis brewing. People are very upset. They don't feel like they can trust the authority of the church anymore. They don't feel they've been genuine, straight-forward: the people they have covered up, the mistakes, priests who have been wayward and abusive. I think there is a real problem structurally with bishops and credibility. I think they've lost a lot of credibility with the ordinary person in the pew.

Roberta: The reverse, the zero-tolerance thing, that didn't give them any more credibility, because I don't think anybody is fighting back very much. They are saying, We are going to do it anyway. It is a real loss of credibility. People, I think, will stop giving. Whatever happens in Boston. Cardinal Law finally, sort of, apologized. People wrote it off as insincere.

Evelyn: He was forced into it. It took him months to do it.

Roberta: Months and months. So we now have a grand jury sitting in session [in Cuyahoga County, Ohio]. Can you believe the banner headline today: 800 cases. This again turns people off.

Evelyn: People are saying the Catholic church needs married priests. Have celibacy be an option rather than be required. Ordain women. This has been talked about in practically every article that you see. Groups like VOTF (Voice of the Faithful) and CTA (Call to Action).

As Dagmar said earlier, the Vatican said that particularly priests are not supposed to talk about ordaining women, because it is not a possibility, it is not going to happen. Actually, more people are talking about it now then they even were when the CDF made that statement!

Parker: We've got about a minute, Dagmar. Do you want to finish?

Dagmar: Denial is a treacherous disease. The addiction is to power!

(end of tape two)

PARTICIPANTS:

Dagmar Braun Celeste is an Austrian-American woman-priest, mother of six children and numerous grandchildren, and former feminist First Lady of Ohio during her marriage to Governor Richard Celeste.

Roberta Steinbacher is a former nun, political activist, professor of urban studies and development officer at Cleveland State University, and former official in the Celeste administration.

Evelyn Elizabeth Hunt is a former nun, affirmative action compliance specialist at Cleveland State University, and president of the board of the national Women's Ordination Conference.

Jacqueline K. Parker is a retired associate professor of social welfare history and policy whose articles have appeared in *Social Service Review, Social Work,* and *NASW Speaks,* and reference books. Her work in oral history includes a U.S. Children's Bureau chief, child welfare and social security experts, and religious subjects. She is a Presbyterian elder.

PROVENANCE:

Taping, November 24, 2002, at Evelyn Hunt's house in Cleveland Heights, Ohio. Present: Dagmar, Roberta, Evelyn, and Jackie Parker, interviewer.

The tapes cover Dagmar's spiritual journey up to the moment on the Danube, buoyed by steadfast and faithful friends, carriers of God's hesed.

This is Part II of Dagmar's personal story. It is interwoven with the stories of Roberta & Evelyn (among other companion of conscience), who were both young women in religious orders during the time of Vatican II, the milk and honey of their formation. Their lives 'dance ahead' and intersect with the growing number whose vocation is to serve Church in 'particular' ministries ('valid but illicit') in western and central Europe and the Americas.

Part II , <u>The Spiritual Journey toward Ordination of Dagmar Celeste</u>, (two 94-minute digital audio tapes) was transcribed (for the first time), edited, and indexed during an intensive period, June 1-8, 2007, by Jacqueline K. Parker in Washington, D.C. and has been reviewed by Dagmar and Evelyn and Roberta.

This slightly shortened edition, 2009, is being made available online under the auspices of Constellation Press, as "<u>The Spiritual Journey toward a Danube 7 Ordination.</u>"

The original versions of <u>Companions of Conscience</u>, Parts I & II, can be found at Kent State University Archives (Ohio) in the manuscript collections of Dagmar Celeste or Evelyn Hunt (under seal). –jkp, 4-20-2009

APPENDIX

Contents

Biographical Sketch of Dagmar Braun Celeste
Collages And Clippings
***NCR* Report on Danube 7 Ordinations**

DAGMAR BRAUN CELESTE: THE FIRST AMERICAN ROMAN CATHOLIC WOMAN PRIEST, 2002

Dagmar Celeste, M.A., is an Austrian-American who grew up in a household of women. Born in 1941 in an ancient town near Vienna, she remembers magical walks along the Danube with her mother or grandmother, searching out red currants and gooseberries, as they spun faery tales for Dagmar and her younger sister.

The war shaped the young, exuberant child of the church within the polyglot context of faded empire: a paternal grandfather, an imperial Habsburg bureaucrat; an uncle, an Aristotle scholar at the University of Vienna. Her father, a lawyer, returned from the war embittered. Her mother and their orchard in Krems helped the household survive the war, the danger of bombings, and the presence of Russian officers encamped in their home in the early part of Allied occupation.

Dagmar was sent by the Red Cross to Trieste at age six as "an undernourished oldest child." Two sisters, a doctor and a teacher, gentled her back to health, to fluency in Italian, and to a precocious grasp of Italian art, sculpture, and music.

At her first communion in Krems, Dagmar experienced a mystical sense that there was a sacred space in her that would always be "virgin." When confirmation followed that summer in Trieste, the knowledge that she was "chosen to be a warrior of the spirit" filled her.

By age ten, the family had moved to Vienna. Resilient Dagmar was eventually entered into the Neuland School where she came under the influence of Dr. Lotte Leitmeyer, the first European woman canon lawyer, who was on faculty of the school and at the University of Vienna. In Dagmar's senior year her class skipped the cultural tour of Italy to visit a shrine devoted to the Mother of God (Maria Zell).

Leitmeyer, subversively, taught her to "trust her inner voice, to be true to her own conscience." Says Dagmar in her book, *'We Can Do Together'* (2002), Leitmeyer was "the original feminist in my life." She encouraged Dagmar to go to Oxford; and she "demanded the will to goodness—even heroic greatness…"

Dagmar's internal meaning-making as she puzzled through dilemmas with mentors and best friends resulted in ethical directions for the rest of her life. "Learning love" is a "balancing act in life that requires perfect pitch." There is comfort, healing, in women's voices; together women "break silence, cushion falls, remember pain, reclaim power."

A Lutheran schoolmate at Neuland, whose family lived in a fin-de-siècle style house, Gustave Klimt on their walls, with arts and crafts furnishings, helped Dagmar recover a love of her mother tongue -- high German with a Viennese dialect – and the pleasure and intimacy of "living with" art, not just on museum walls.

At Oxford to study for the Cambridge English language exams Dagmar met a young American, Richard Celeste, the love of her life. As his spouse they "did together" what neither thought would have been possible separately. Their trajectory together took them to India (and the mentoring friendships of Ambassador Chester Bowles and Dorothy Stebbins); six children, and two terms in the Governor's house in Columbus, Ohio. As "first lady of Ohio" Dagmar followed the Viennese template and Steb Bowles' example in India; she introduced contemporary American art and artists. And beyond the aesthetic, Dagmar framed the political in social justice terms. She developed a First Lady's Cabinet or "core circle" that birthed women's leadership, networking, and programming throughout the state agencies [1983-1991]. One of their singular social justice accomplishments resulted in the governor's pardon of several "battered women" who had in desperation killed their abusers.

During this time, Dagmar lived out a new sense of herself—always, first as Mother. But with the hard birth of a sixth child, and post-partum depression, a new necessity emerged and flourished in the creation of structures that, collectively, sustain and nourish women.

In the late 1980s, Dagmar joined the board of Mary's Pence, whose aim is to use money "to transform anger about the church's neglect of women into positive action, and to participate in recovering *our* church by empowering women in need of help and healing." Earlier she worked with Cleveland's professional women to make feminist advocacy groups, WomenSpace and Sacred Space creative going-concerns.

In her mid-fifties Dagmar was shaken by divorce. This seemed to propel her into another emancipatory transformation—to *reclaim* the sacred space within herself and fill it with a priestly response to God's ever present call.

The Vatican's subsequent excommunication, after the Seven Women were ordained on the Danube in June 2002, she has accepted as the *price of her freedom* to minister to "women and children, those rejected, dejected, addicted, and those locked in state prison cells or in prisons of their own making."

Living with the paradox that the church into which she was born "distorts the goodness of Jesus Christ, who lived and died to free us for loving," Dagmar's is a ministry of reconciliation. Her vehicles are a retreat house on Kelleys Island on Lake Erie, a nonprofit, Tyrian, an annual Brigidfest, and her own design of an urban ashram, Oasis House, on the west side of Cleveland. Their aim is together to work to restore the *spirit of creativity, healing, and peace* among those who, out of their complexity, or pain, seek goodness.

Jacqueline K. Parker, Interviewer and Editor
Washington, D.C. April 2009

COLLAGES AND CLIPPINGS

15 When they had broken their fast, Jesus said to Simon Peter, Simon, son of Jonah, do you love me more than these things? He said to him, Yes, my Lord, you know that I love you. Jesus said to him, Feed my lambs.

16 He said to him again the second time, Simon, son of Jonah, do you love me? He said to him, Yes, my Lord, you know that I love you. Jesus said to him, Feed my sheep.

17 He said to him again the third time, Simon, son of Jonah, do you love me? It grieved Peter because he said to him the third time, Do you love me? So he said to him, My Lord, you understand well everything, you know that I love you. Jesus said to him, Feed my ewes.
— John 21:15-17, Lamsa Translation

Altar created by Dagmar and Evelyn on retreat during the discerment process on the spiritual journey toward ordination of Rev. Dagmar Braun Celeste. Gospel reading of ordination mass of Danube 7.

Dagmar Braun Celeste on retreat during the discernment process to become ordained.

Gathering of Cleveland Faithful:
L=R: Dagmar Braun Celeste, Evelyn Hunt, Carolyn Hilter, Linda DeBor, Maureen Brett, Kay Eaton.

Roberta Steinbacher and Dagmar Celeste at the Venus of Willendorf, paleolithic site near Krems, Austria.

Seven women to be ordained: Iris Muller, Ida Raming, Pia Brunner, Dagmar Braun Celeste, Sr. Adeline Roitinger, Gisela Forster, and Christine Mayr–Lumetzberger.

Bishop Romulo Braschi laying hands on Dagmar Braun Celeste as ordination takes place on the Danube River, June 29, 2002. NCR reporter, John Allen, in background

Young
altar
server
incensing
women to
be
ordained.

Rev. Celeste shares
communion with Elli,
sister of Christine
Mayr–Lumetzberger.

Bishop Rafael
Regelsberger
hands the cup to
Rev. Celeste at the
ordination mass.

On the boat on the Danube River, seven women were ordained Roman Catholic priests on June 29, 2002

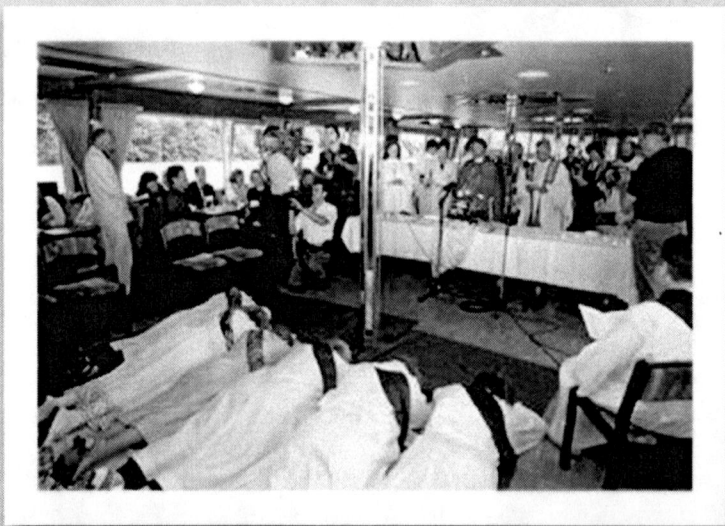

Prostrated before the altar and before God, the Danube 7 women prepare to take vows as Roman Catholic priests.

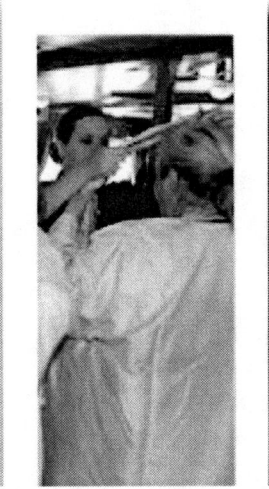

Eleanor, Rev. Celeste's oldest granddaughter, helps her with vestiture at the ordination.

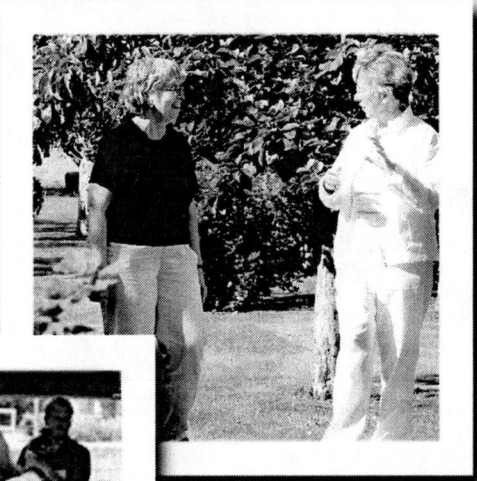

Evelyn Hunt and Bishop Christine Mayr-Lumetzberger

Bishop Braschi congratulates Rev. Dagmar Braun Celeste following ordination.

"From ugly duckling to strong swan."
—Dagmar Celeste

109

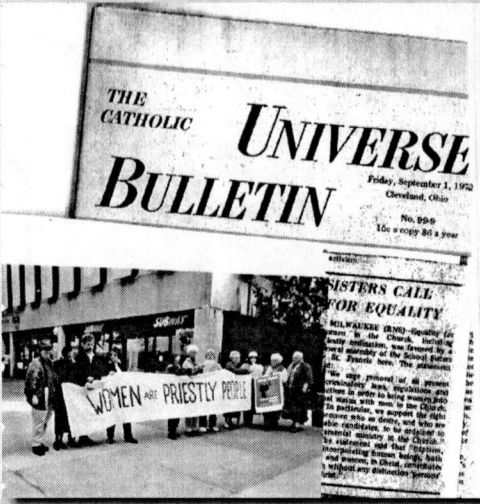

Cleveland Women's Ordination Conference representatives at their yearly prayer service outside St. John's Cathedral at the all male ordination.

Jacqueline K. Parker and Evelyn Hunt, Las Cruces, NM, 1994

Bishop Christine Mayr–Lumetzberger and Rev. Dagmar Braun Celeste with the Danube in the background.

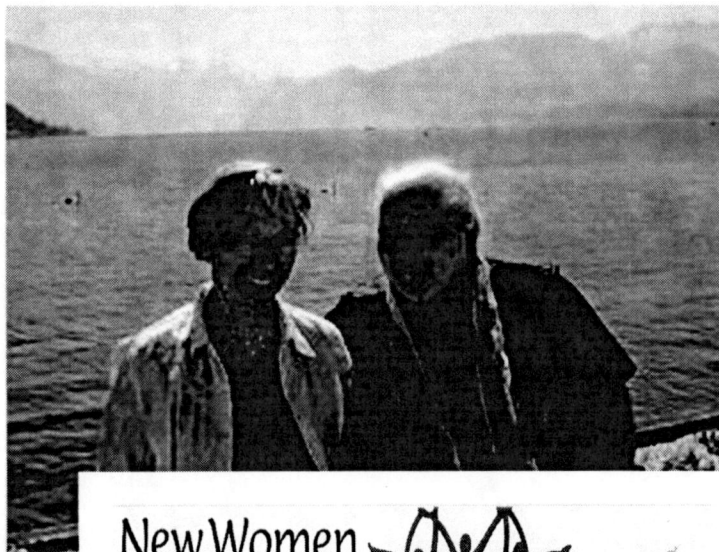

New Women New Church

WOMEN'S ORDINATION CONFERENCE

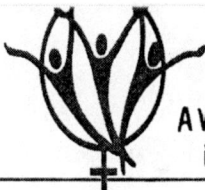

A Voice for Women in the Church

VOL. 26, NO. 2

SUMMER 2003

One Year Later, Two Women Ordained as Bishops

Gisela Forster (left) and Christine Mayr-Lumetzberger (right) are pictured here at their priestly ordination June 29, 2003. On the anniversary of their ordination, both were consecrated as bishops in a service that took place secretly.

NCR ONLINE: SEVEN WOMEN "ORDAINED" PRIESTS, JUNE 29 (2002)

In ceremony they term "not licit, but a fact"

By JOHN L. ALLEN JR.
Passau, Germany

Champions of the ordination of women as Roman Catholic priests have long dreamt of presenting the world with a *fait accompli*: women ordained by legitimate Catholic bishops in defiance of Vatican opposition. Rather than waiting for permission, a "top down" solution that under John Paul II seems ever more improbable, change would thus come from the "bottom up."

On a gorgeous Bavarian summer day June 29, aboard a specially chartered pleasure boat on the Danube River, seven Catholic women and two bishops who are not in communion with Rome, but who claim to stand in apostolic succession, tried to translate that dream into reality. Four Germans, two Austrians and one American were ordained before some 200 family, friends, supporters and journalists, on the feast of Sts. Peter and Paul.

According to the women, the ball is now in Rome's court.

"It is not a licit solution, but it is a fact," said Christine Mayr-Lumetzberger, one of the seven. "We have to live *with* this fact and *in* this fact."

Church authorities rejected both the credentials of the bishops and the validity of the ordinations, based on the teaching that the Catholic church has no power to ordain women as priests.

How the outcome will be judged in the court of Catholic public opinion, however, remains to be seen.

A spokesperson for the U.S.-based Women's Ordination Conference told *NCR* that a group of American Catholic women hope to stage a similar event shortly in the United States.

The seven women claiming ordination June 29 were: Germans Iris Müller, Ida Raming, Gisela Forster, and Pia Brunner; Austrians Mayr-Lumetzberger and School Sr. Adelinde Theresia Roitinger; and an Austrian-born American who used the assumed name of "Angela White."

From left to right: Iris Müller, Ida Raming, Gisela Forster and Christine Mayr-Lumetzberger.
photos by -- John L. Allen Jr.

The women said they had followed a three-year program of theological and spiritual preparation.

114

The man presented as presiding bishop was 61-year-old Argentine Romulo Braschi, a former Catholic priest whose checkered background has raised question marks.

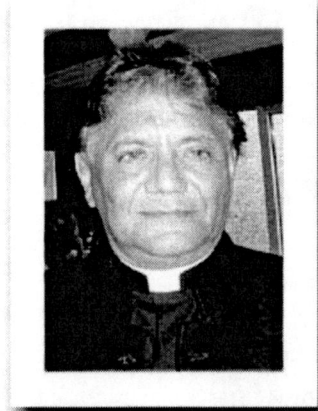

Romulo Braschi

Braschi claims to have been ordained a bishop twice: once by fellow Argentine Roberto Padin in 1998, described as a prelate in the breakaway "Catholic-Apostolic Church of Brasil," and again by Jeronimo Podestá in January 1999.

In Podestá's case at least, there is no doubt as to his own legitimacy. He served as bishop of the Avellanda diocese in Argentina from 1962 to 1967, before being removed for alleged excesses in pushing social action and church reform. He went on to become a supporter of optional clerical celibacy, and died on June 24, 2000.

Skeptics, however, say that Podestá never supported the splinter church founded by Braschi, and hence they doubt that he ever performed the ordination. Braschi appeared at a press conference on June 29, however, with a notarized document from his lawyer in Buenos Aires, which he said attests to the event.

In reality, Braschi's episcopal status makes no theological difference, since official Catholic doctrine holds that it is impossible to ordain a woman no matter who performs the ritual. Politically, however, the challenge to that doctrine would be more dramatic if it came from a legitimate bishop.

Local church authorities thus wasted little time in making clear that, from their point of view, Braschi does not fall into that category.

A spokesperson for the Munich archdiocese called him a "charlatan" in a June 26 statement, stating that he was excommunicated in the 1970s and that his claim to apostolic succession rests on "venturesome assertions."

The statement noted that Braschi today describes himself as bishop of the "Catholic-Apostolic Church of Jesus the King," which he founded in the 1970s. Braschi claims 250 followers in Switzerland and Germany, though the archdiocese put the number at 50. In 1996, Braschi launched something called the "Charismatic-Oxala-Nana Union" in Munich, devoted to "Afro-Argentinian nature religion." He is also said to have embraced the Hindu doctrine of karma.

Braschi previously ordained his wife, Alicia Carbera Braschi, as a priest. She joined him in the June 29 ordination ritual, wearing liturgical vestments and carrying a crozier.

The other bishop June 29 was Ferdinand Regelsberger, a former Benedictine monk consecrated by Braschi on May 9, 2002, and whose claim to episcopal status thus rests on Braschi's.

While organizers declared themselves satisfied with Braschi's credentials, they acknowledged they had also expected a third bishop, a Czech, who allegedly ordained a handful of women as deacons in secret on Palm Sunday. Though she would not name the bishop, Mayr-Lumetzberger said the women ordained June 29 plan to ask him to re-ordain them in secret, *sub conditionis* -- a technical term meaning that the second ordination would be valid only if the first one is not.

This concern for the fine points of canon law struck some observers as ironic, given that it came in the context of an ordination that openly defied church teaching, and a Mass which included clergy of the Lutheran and Old Catholic churches as concelebrants (also prohibited). Yet participants were in deadly earnest. At one point Braschi read a prayer in Spanish that referred to *hermanos*, "brothers." Someone in the crowd called out "and *hermanas*," or "sisters," whereupon Braschi wheeled sharply and said: "Today we follow the Roman rite."

The women stressed they do not intend to separate from the Catholic church. "We don't want a fight with the church,"

Forster said at the press conference. "This is a sign of renewal *for* the church, not *against* it."

Reaction from officialdom was nonetheless negative.

Bishop Maximilian Aichern of Linz, Austria, sent a letter June 28 to Mary-Lumetzberger, who lives in Aichern's diocese, threatening excommunication and interdict if she went ahead. A spokesperson for Cardinal Friedrich Wetter of Munich called the event a "sectarian spectacle" that had "nothing to do with the Catholic church."

Cardinal Joachim Mesiner of Cologne said the project was absurd, comparing a woman wanting to be a priest with a man wanting to give birth. Roitinger told reporters that she has been threatened with expulsion from her religious order, the School Sisters of Hallein.

The sour notes were, however, not restricted to church officials. "These women are not representative of most Catholics here," said Otto Schwankl, dean of the Catholic theology faculty at the University of Passau, in a June 27 interview with *NCR*. "Most people think it's nonsense."

Even some groups supportive of women's ordination expressed reservations.

The Austrian branch of the "We Are Church" reform group, the "Church from Below" movement in Germany, the www.womenpriests.org web site, and the New Wine movement in England all discouraged the June 29 event. The argument for women priests should be made, they said, from within the Catholic mainstream.

On the other hand, delegates from the U.S.-based Womens Ordination Conference and the Canadian "Catholic Network for Women's Equality" were on hand to offer support.

The driving force behind the event was Mayr-Lumetzberger, 46. Raming and Müller were acknowledged as inspirational leaders. Both now in their 70s, they said a sense of time running short was part of the motivation.

"We have been very patient for 40 years," Raming told *NCR*, saying that she and Müller submitted a petition to the Second Vatican Council in 1963 seeking discussion of women's ordination, and have been working on the issue ever since.

Some progressive critics noted that since Vatican II Catholic theology has emphasized that it is always a local community that calls forth a vocation, and the seven women ordained June 29 have no such base of support. But Raming said the analysis does not apply. "You cannot ask that we have a community like a regular priest," she said. "We have an extraordinary situation."

Mayr-Lumetzberger said she would begin celebrating Mass in a private chapel in her home, and will build her own community.

"I will go with people on their way to God, pray with them and celebrate with them," she said. "I will prepare women for

119

ministry. Otherwise, I'm as teacher at my school and I am a priestly person in my everyday work."

The ordinations were preceded by months of tantalizing, and at times baffling, secrecy.

A small group of reporters invited to witness the ordinations was instructed to show up in a parking lot in Passau, Germany, at 8:30 am on the 29th. Not until then was it made clear that the event would take place on board the *MS Passau.*

Organizers refused to confirm the identities of either the bishops or the participants until the moment the ceremony began, and in fact the final line-up of women was not finalized until shortly beforehand.

At one stage up to four Americans planned to take part, though all but one withdrew on the grounds that they were not part of the three-year process of preparation.

The lone American who went ahead did so under a false name. She declined an *NCR* request for comment, though she contributed an essay recounting her personal story to a book entitled *We Are Women Priests*, published in German and distributed at the press conference. The essay contains more than enough information to establish her identity for the truly curious.

Despite the precautions, the day was not free of vitriol. At the press conference, an Austrian conservative who publishes a small local newspaper repeatedly challenged the women and Braschi. Frustrated with their responses, he baited Mayr-Lumtezberger by blurting out: "You have nice breasts and I would like to see you sunbathe naked!" Security guards moved in, triggering a brief uproar. The man eventually returned to his seat.

On the boat itself, the ceremony featured a few oddly post-modern flourishes, such as a Paraguyan folk band belting out an instrumental version of Simon and Garfunkel's "The Sound of Silence" as a lead-in to the "Our Father."

Aside from these occasional flashes of the surreal, however, most observers seemed enthusiastic. Johnson called the June 29 ordinations a "model" for American action.

Carol Crowley, one of the American women who decided not to go through with ordination this time, said she was looking forward to doing something similar back home.

"Some say 'Next year in Jerusalem!" Crowley said. "But I say, 'Next year in the United States!"

John L. Allen Jr. is NCR's Vatican correspondent. His e-mail address is jallen@natcath.org. National Catholic Reporter, posted July 1, 2002

END NOTES

[1] Mairéad Corrigan-Maguire and Betty Williams, founders of the Northern Ireland Peace Movement (aka the Community of Peace People) were awarded the Nobel Peace Prize in 1976. *See also* Mairéad's (1999) *Vision of peace: Faith and hope in Northern Ireland*, ed. by John Dear (Maryknoll, NY: Orbis).

[2] From a Croatian-Irish-Catholic heritage, and graduate of Case Western Reserve University, Kucinich served a 'tumultuous' term as mayor of Cleveland in the late 1970s. In 1985 he ran briefly as an Independent candidate for governor against Democrat Richard Celeste. By 1996, he won a political upset against a Republican incumbent to represent the 10th Congressional District (western Cleveland) in the U.S. House of Representatives. He's a member of the Congressional Progressive Caucus, an ardent peace activist, and twice has thrown his hat into the Presidential ring (2004, 2008). From *Wikipedia* online.

[3] J. Phillip Newell (1999). *The book of creation: An introduction to Celtic spirituality.* (Mahwah, NJ: Paulist Press). Newell is a Church of Scotland minister whose book "places the Celtic church and tradition in the context of the wider church, both Catholic and Protestant....[It treats] each of the seven days of creation, through themes of light, wildness, fecundity, harmony, creatureliness [sic], image, and stillness.[ending each chapter] with an exercise of meditation based on centering prayer. The sources for this spiritual gem come from the Bible and the works of Celtic Christians from Pelagius and Eriugena through George MacDonald, ... including materials from the Carmina Gadelica." From an Amazon online review by Michael Foret (1 Dec. 2000).

[4] *See* Patricia Lefevere (1 Mar. 2002). "Margaret Traxler lived her passion for justice: teacher marched in Selma, carried a banner in St. Peter's Square: An appreciation." In *National Catholic Reporter.*

Traxler (1924-2002) entered the order of the School Sisters of Notre Dame as a teenager during World War II. After participating in the Selma civil rights march with Martin Luther King, Jr. in 1965, her social justice energies found institutional focus as educational director of the National Catholic Conference for Interracial Justice in Chicago.

From this base the "traveling workshops," then-sister Roberta Steinbacher refers to in the text, began. By 1969 Traxler's connection with grass-roots nuns coalesced into the formation of the National Coalition of American Nuns (NCAN), 1,800-strong at her death.

Her participation in the protest at St. Peter's Square in 1994, while the Bishops' Synod on Religious Life met [holding the banner mentioned in the text], resulted in her detention by the Italian police.

Lefevere mentions that Traxler 'came into her own' after age 50, when her Institute of Women Today came about. Her activities highlighted peace in Northern Ireland, cofounding the Interreligious Conference on Soviet Jewry, etc. When offered a position in the Jimmy Carter administration (as an undersecretary of Education), she declined in order to continue her focus on work with women in prison.

Traxler's papers are deposited in the Special Collections of Marquette University.

[5] Wells became a federal judge on the U.S. District Court, Northern District of Ohio (nominated by President Bill Clinton). In the 1980s and 1990s Wells also taught (adjunct assistant professor at the College of Urban Affairs, Cleveland State University) while serving as judge on the Court of Common Pleas of Cuyahoga County (1983-1994). Roberta Steinbacher (with time-out in the cabinet of Gov. Celeste) worked with Wells at CSU. Roberta is professor of Urban Studies and assistant dean for program development at CSU.

[6] Frank Murphy was appointed auxiliary bishop of Baltimore by Pope Paul VI (1976). The genesis of his support for women's ordination is described in *NCR*: "While dining with friends, he found himself explaining the discipline of celibacy, which called for avoiding friendships with women 'since such relationship did not benefit my ministry nor allow me to be as free as possible for the good of the kingdom of God'. He was surprised when a woman in the group said she was 'profoundly offended' because his remarks made her feel inferior. She resented being seen as a threat to his vocation rather than a potential colleague in the fulfillment of it. Her comments were a turning point ..." At the 1978 National Conference of Catholic Bishops meeting in Chicago, Murphy for the first time broached this topic on the floor.
   See Retta Blaney (27 Aug. 1999). "Bishop Murphy, 'total mensch', fights cancer." *National Catholic Reporter.*

[7] "Bishop Frank Murphy Scholarship for Women in Ministry." Two or more $1,000 scholarship are awarded "to female WOC members who are furthering their theological education. Women in seminary and diocesan certificate programs are also encouraged to apply." *See* http://www.womensordination.org

[8] Donald B. Cozzens (2002). *Sacred silence: Denial & the crisis in the church.* (Collegeville, MN: Liturgical Press). Since then Cozzens has published (2004) *Faith that dares to speak* and (2006) *Freeing celibacy* (also through the Liturgical Press). Dagmar & Evelyn occasionally join Cozzens & other Catholic intellectuals at the CWRU campus *Arabica* café for Saturday morning discussions on current issues.

[9] Barbara Ferraro & Patricia Hussey, with Jane O'Reilly. (1990). *No turning back: Two nuns battle with the Vatican over women's right to choose* . (NY: Poseidon Press).

[10] Sister Jeannine Gramick and Father Robert Nugent were eventually silenced by the Congregation for the Doctrine of the Faith [during Cardinal Ratzinger's tenure] for their pastoral ministry to Catholic homosexuals. Sister as a matter of conscience did not obey. *See* NCR online, for its extensive documentation of the "Gramick/Nugent Case, 1988-1999" including their responses to the CDF's assertion of errors in the Gramick/Nugent 1992 book, *Building bridges: Gay & lesbian reality & the Catholic church* (Mystic, CT: Twenty-Third Publications). Margaret Traxler & Donna Quinn issued a press release (7/18/99) calling on American bishops to appeal the ruling.

[11] *See, for instance* (1995). *Luke;* (1999) *Wisdom's friends: Community and christology in the Fourth Gospel;* and Carol A. Newsom & Sharon H. Ringe, eds. (1992/1998). *Women's bible commentary.* (all Louisville: Westminster John Knox Press).

[12] Ludmila (a female priest) was secretly ordained in Communist Czechoslovakia in 1970 after the "Prague Spring" by underground bishop Felix Maria Davidek. *See* Wikipedia online.

[13] Dagmar Braun Celeste (2002). *We can do together: Impressions of a recovering feminist first lady.* (Kent, Ohio: Kent State University).

[14] Frank Bruni (6 Aug. 2002). "Vatican: Female 'priests' excommunicated." *New York Times.*

[15] *See New York Times* (6-30-2002). 7 women are ordained; *and* John Allen in *National Catholic Reporte* (7-1-2002).

[16] Werner Ertel & Gisela Forster (2002). *Wir sind Priesterinnen: Aus aktuellem Anlass: Die Weihe von Frauen 2002* (Dusseldorf: Patmos Verlag Gmbh & Co. KG). German edition withdrawn & destroyed.- jkp

LaVergne, TN USA
09 September 2009
157237LV00002B/89/P